D0931692

In this special edition of *American Century*, readers have a unique opportunity to review retailing's service to consumers during one hundred years of changing American life styles.

Each of those one hundred years, from 1872 to 1972, was a seedbed of change and challenge. It was an exhilarating—and occasionally exasperating—period for American consumers and those who served them. Some years were kinder than others, yet each held its own special significance for people, institutions, and the nation.

The contrasts between the 1870's and the 1970's are obvious. The similarities are not so apparent, but they are important. Consumers still are seeking and expecting better merchandise values and improved services. Such demands one hundred years ago prompted a twenty-eight-year-old by the name of Aaron Montgomery Ward to develop an entirely new system of meeting the needs of rural Americans. He adopted a revolutionary policy, "Satisfaction Guaranteed or Your Money Back," to assure consumers that he was trustworthy. He developed among his customers confidence in his integrity as a merchant as well as confidence in his merchandise.

Today, better educated, more affluent, and more discriminating customers are continuing to upgrade their expectations. By 1980 more than half of all American households will have annual incomes of more than $10,000, compared with 37 per cent today. There will be 33 million college-trained consumers, compared with 20 million today, shopping for goods and services. Thus, the 1970's will be distinctly different from even the 1960's as businesses plan for consumer needs and wants and anticipate their demands.

Montgomery Ward's centennial year of 1972 was a launching pad for scores of new, improved, and exciting products and services, presented in an environment providing consumers with the convenience and comfort they have a right to expect from major national retail merchandisers.

The challenges and opportunities of the seventies and beyond are greater than ever for all retailers. Yet, even as we move ahead through the seventies, with all its anticipated improvements in services, we daily reaffirm in millions of individual transactions our one-hundred-year-old credo of "Satisfaction Guaranteed" as the best of all possible protections for all consumers.

E. S. Donnell

President, Montgomery Ward & Co.

The Founding Years

The founder of the one-hundred-year-old mail-order industry was Aaron Montgomery Ward, who was born February 17, 1844, in New Jersey. He was nine years old when his parents moved west to Niles, Michigan, where his father became a cobbler. Young Aaron left school at fourteen to be an apprentice, then did a man's work in a stave factory for twenty-five cents a day, and later stacked brick for thirty cents a day.

He went to the county seat, St. Joseph, and got a job in a shoe store. There he learned small-town retailing—selling to people he knew—and rose to head clerk and general manager, remaining at the store for three years.

In 1866 Ward boarded one of the steamboats making daily runs across Lake Michigan to Chicago. His first job there was as a clerk for Field, Palmer and Leiter, forerunner of Marshall Field & Co. Later he sold dry goods in Illinois, Iowa, and Missouri.

In the tedious round of train trips to rural communities—hiring rigs at the local livery stables, driving out to crossroads stores, and listening to the complaints of the back-country proprietors and their rural customers—he conceived a new merchandising technique: selling to the country people direct by mail.

It was a time when rural consumers longed for the comforts of city folk, yet all too often were victimized by monopolists and overcharged

Aaron Montgomery Ward, 1844–1913

Ward's first catalogues were single-sheet price lists.

The young firm occupied the second floor of this building on Kinzie Street in 1874.

George R. Thorne, 1837–1918

Nebraska farm family of the 1880's pose before sod home. Material for the mother's dress and boys' blouses came from "a bolt of Montgomery Ward calico."

by the costs of the many middlemen then required to bring manufactured products to the countryside. The quality of merchandise also was suspect in those days, and the hapless farmer had no recourse in a *caveat emptor* economy.

Although his idea was generally considered to border on lunacy and his first inventory was destroyed by the Great Chicago Fire of 1871, Ward persevered until, in August of 1872, he distributed his first single-sheet price list offering merchandise to farmers and ranchers throughout the Midwest.

The young firm got off to a slow start, but Ward fortunately acquired a partner in his brother-in-law, George R. Thorne, and their enterprise weathered the panic of 1873. As Ward's skeptical country customers learned that the catalogue did, indeed, offer them quality merchandise at lower prices, sales rapidly increased.

Many years later Ward's catalogue was copied by other enterprising mechants, most notably Richard W. Sears and Alvah C. Roebuck, who mailed their first general catalogue in 1896. Others entered the field, and by 1972 catalogue sales alone exceeded $3 billion. In addition, between 3,000 and 4,000 direct-mail firms and an even greater number of individual entrepreneurs today offer almost every conceivable form of merchandise to consumers through the mail.

Aaron Montgomery Ward contributed more than technique to American business. He contributed a philosophy as well, an attitude of devotion to personalized customer service that was just as revolutionary in its time as the idea of selling goods by mail.

Although the word "consumerism" has a modern ring to it, it was consumer protection that prompted Aaron Montgomery Ward to start his catalogue business.

3

This illustration from the 1880 catalogue showed bill clerks, examiners, sorters, packers, and (inset) the grocery department. Proud of its efficiency, the young firm included several such scenes in early catalogues.

3½" x 5½"
1876

5¾" x 8½"
1878

3¾" x 7"
1877

8¾" x 11"
1893

From the pocket-sized volume of 1875, the catalogue grew to a two-pound, 544-page book in 1893.

The National Grange of the Patrons of Husbandry was formed in 1867, and farmers saw it as a cooperative means of fighting the high cost of supplies. It was the Grange membership of nearly half a million discontented consumers that Ward had in mind when he issued his first catalogue. And he acknowledged the importance of Grangers to his success in his 1876 catalogue with this statement: "When we introduced our system in 1872, we were looked upon with scorn by the monopolists and suspicion by the Patrons themselves. In the short period of three years we have saved the consumers directly over one million dollars and indirectly millions by breaking up monopolies and forcing dealers to sell their goods at fair prices. This herculean task has been accomplished through the power of the Grange organization."

Having found in consumerism the inspiration for a whole new way of doing business, Aaron Montgomery Ward went on to make still another contribution to the fundamental buyer-seller relationship. One of the earliest landmarks in consumerism was established when this statement appeared in Ward's Catalogue No. 13, dated 1875:

We Guarantee All of Our Goods.

If any of them are not satisfactory after due inspection, we will take them back, pay all expenses, and refund the money paid for them. When in the city please call and see us.

MONTGOMERY WARD & CO.

This policy, which set a standard of excellence in consumer relations for American business as a whole, did much to condition the

American public to expect quality merchandise and service as well as fair play from every business enterprise. It tolled the death knell for the age-old merchant precept of *caveat emptor*. Backing up this policy, which has been adopted almost universally by American businesses, are billions of dollars' worth of market research, product development, quality control, protective packaging, informative labeling, and efficient distribution methods that combine to provide the American public with the highest standard of living in the world.

Ward was convinced that American consumers wanted good quality merchandise. During the depression years following the panic of 1893, many manufacturers catered to the majority of people who could not make ends meet by producing what the Ward catalogue described as "cheap worthless goods of the most disgraceful quality which were put upon the market by not-over-particular merchants at glittering prices."

Ward's policy was unshaken: sacrifice of quality to the point of not giving satisfaction made an article worthless, however low the price. Ward told his buyers, "The ever-growing trade we enjoy proves that, after all, the people of the country are not such fools as some merchants and manufacturers seem to think they are."

In addition to his role as a pioneering merchant and consumerist, Aaron Montgomery Ward also earned recognition as one of the nation's first environmentalists.

Chicago's lakefront in 1890 was not a pretty sight. Contemporary observers reported livery stables, squatters' shacks, and mountains of cans, ashes, and garbage. Ward's firm had recently occupied new quarters on the west side of Michigan Avenue, directly across the street from the dismal lakefront.

Scaffolding erected by the city for loading garbage and street sweepings into railroad cars prompted Ward in 1890 to take the first step in a legal war that was to last twenty years and cost him a substantial fortune as well as the friendship of many of Chicago's most prominent citizens.

It took seven years to settle Ward's first court battle, and three more were to follow, each occasioned by some building proposal that encroached upon Chicago citizens' rights to a lakefront park.

Ward was characterized as "stubborn and eccentric," his litigation as "a horrible example of the triumph of legal red tape," and "a public misfortune." He was "chief obstructionist," acting on "whim or caprice" and "not in good faith." The Watchdog of the Lakefront, as the newspapers called him, was seen barking for his own interest with an eye to compensation by condemnation.

The famous Ward Tower, at 385 feet the tallest building west of the Alleghenies, was completed in 1899. It dominated the block-long building on Chicago's Michigan Avenue and the splendid view from its observation tower attracted thousands of tourists.

Shortly before his death, Ward said, "I fought for the poor people of Chicago, not for the millionaires. Here is a park frontage on the lake, comparing favorably with the Bay of Naples, which city officials would crowd with buildings, transforming the breathing spot for the poor into a show ground of the educated rich. I do not think it is right. . . ."

A *Chicago Tribune* editorial after his death in 1913 recalled that Ward had been criticized unjustly: "We know now that Mr. Ward was right, was foresighted, was public spirited."

Additional recognition came last year when the Ward company announced the establishment, in honor of its founder, of the nation's first major public library collection of environmental literature and art. The *Chicago Daily News* editorialized that the city's "dedicated environmentalists had a distinguished predecessor in Aaron Montgomery Ward," and Mayor Richard J. Daley described the collection as "a fitting memorial to the man who alone saved Grant Park for future generations."

If you had told Aaron Montgomery Ward that he was a "pioneering merchant" whose ideas would lead to a multi-billion-dollar industry, he certainly would have welcomed your enthusiasm, although even he might have questioned such a gigantic sales volume because such numbers were fantastic one hundred years ago.

If you had called him a consumerist, he patiently would have explained that satisfying customers was the only way he knew to conduct a successful catalogue business.

If you had told him he was one of the nation's first environmentalists, he would have replied that he was simply trying to preserve "a breathing spot" for the people.

However you describe him, Aaron Montgomery Ward, and the mass distribution mail-order industry he founded, truly made significant contributions to improvement of life styles of millions of families.

In 1906 a Ward company publication carried these photos of the lakefront area and editorialized: "The site of the park, which is within pistol shot of our building, resembles more the Bad Lands of the West than a modern park." Ward Tower dominates skyline.

The Middle Years

Although they adopted a daughter, Marjorie, the Wards were otherwise childless, and in time their five nephews, Charles Thorne's sons, entered the business. By 1893 the Thorne family managed the firm, although Ward held the title of president until his death. Beginning in 1893, therefore, the company was dominated by the Thorne family, an influence that was to continue until 1919, when the firm became a public corporation.

Thorne brothers (from left): Robert, William, Charles, George, and James

It was in this period that the catalogue industry truly came of age and became firmly interwoven in the fabric of the nation's economic and cultural pattern. It was the Thorne brothers who carried to national expansion the mail-order idea of Aaron Montgomery Ward.

Shortly after the turn of the century, the company established branches in Kansas City, Portland, and St. Paul and built a mammoth new plant on the banks of the Chicago River. The catalogue itself developed rapidly, not only in size but in techniques of presentation. Indeed, the mail-order catalogue was the vehicle for introducing many new developments in the graphic arts.

The first commercial use of the patent binding process was for the Ward catalogue of 1896, an edition that also included four pages of halftone photographs showing baby bonnets and corsets worn by "live models!" Curtains, portières, and carpets were shown in color photographs in 1899, when the Ward catalogue also represented the first commercial use of rotary printing presses.

The company's interest extended beyond the immediate objective of service to the consumer. The management instituted employee benefit programs that included medical and dental care and offered midmorning breaks where malted milk was provided at no cost to employees. In 1912 Wards became the first major firm to purchase a group life insurance program for employees.

The industry flourished with the development of new postal services. As early as 1895 the Chicago postmaster told a banquet audience that "the largest patron of the Post Office Department is here in Chicago, Montgomery Ward & Co."—a distinction the company was to maintain for many years.

Catalogue distribution was vitally stimulated by the advent of rural free delivery in 1896, and when parcel post service was established in 1913, Wards rushed forty bags of packages to the post office to be first with parcel post in Chicago. The Ward catalogue hailed "Uncle Sam's new delivery service . . . to your very porch step" as being "ideal when you're in a hurry." The hat, dress, or shoes ordered at the last moment would arrive "in time for church next Sunday."

By the beginning of the new century, the mail-order business had become firmly established in the shopping patterns of the nation's consumers. "The Wish Book" was kept handy in the farmer's kitchen, and when a new edition arrived, the old one was given to the children, who cut it up to make paper dolls. Rural schoolteachers found the catalogue invaluable in teaching arithmetic and spelling.

Halftone illustrations were introduced in 1896 catalogue.

1904 catalogue cover portrayed rural free delivery service, which was inaugurated in 1896.

The very life styles of America were altered by catalogue merchandising. Not only material but social and cultural aspects of American life were deeply affected, so much so that in 1946 the Grolier Society included the Montgomery Ward catalogue in its collection of one hundred American books chosen for their impact on the life and culture of the people.

The company recognized—and welcomed—consumer groups who wished to verify that Ward merchandise was all it was claimed to be. When the booming mail-order business fueled the indignation of small-town merchants shortly after the turn of the century, charges were made that the catalogue firms dealt in trashy merchandise. A delegation from the Farmer's Institute of Pocahontas County, Iowa, was invited to Chicago and given free access to the entire Ward establishment to open packages, measure, weigh, and test. They applied acid to fabrics, cut harness, and pounded stove lids.

"We went after the essentials and the lines most attacked by the papers," the committee reported, "and proved to our perfect satisfaction, and we hope to the satisfaction of our Institute members, that the quality of their goods is the same as or better than the qualities that the usual stores sell and that no attack on their quality is justified by the facts."

World War I, with its problems of inflation, scarcity of goods, and the loss of experienced employees to military service, put a damper on the firm's growth. In 1919 control of the firm passed to a group of New York bankers when a new corporation was formed and stock was sold to the public.

Wards was the first Chicago firm to use the parcel post service, introduced in 1913. Parcels in the Chicago mail-order house were chuted from the packing floor to the shipping room.

The Plymouth, Indiana, catalogue "display" unit became Ward's first pilot retail store in 1926.

Postwar depression hit Wards, along with other retail businesses. American life was being transformed, however, and not merely by the war. A sign of the times was the 1922 catalogue's listings of buggy parts but no buggies, while twenty-one pages were devoted to automobile parts and accessories, including Ward's Riverside tires carrying a ten-thousand-mile guarantee. The automobile was changing the buying habits of Ward customers: they were no longer content to purchase just from a catalogue; they wanted to drive to town and see the goods for themselves. New merchandising techniques were required to respond to new customer patterns.

One approach was to establish "merchandise exhibits" where samples of catalogue goods were shown but not sold. When the first of these exhibits opened in Marysville, Kansas, on August 14, 1926, the crowds of people who came from great distances around the countryside went away disappointed and even irritated. They wanted to buy what they saw. Then, when a similar exhibit opened a few months later at Plymouth, Indiana, a carpenter insisted on buying the saw on display. The manager finally gave in, and soon all the "display" merchandise was sold. Wards was in the retail business.

By the end of 1928 Wards had well over 200 retail stores, which accounted for most of the company's nearly $20 million sales increase that year. Retail expansion continued, concentrated in small towns across the nation, and by the end of 1929 Wards had opened 531 retail stores. But the same year also brought the stock market crash and the beginning of the Great Depression.

Mail-order sales plummeted due to fewer—and smaller—orders. In 1931 the company reported an operating loss, and Sewell Lee Avery

By the end of 1929, Wards had opened 531 retail stores, many of them multistory operations similar to this one in Birmingham, Alabama.

9

Refusing to concede his rights when the Army took over the company in 1944, Sewell Avery was carried bodily from the premises.

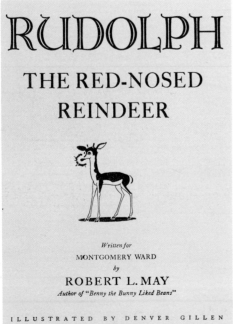

"Rudolph the Red-Nosed Reindeer," the creation of Ward copywriter Robert May in 1939, has become part of American folklore.

was brought in as chief executive officer to save the company from bankruptcy. Avery's moves reversed the four-year declining sales trend and produced a modest profit in 1934. In 1935 he removed the brakes from expansion programs, and during the next seven years opened 178 new stores.

Avery's confidence and determination are credited with bringing the company safely through the thirties. The same grit and single-mindedness also carried him through a now-historic battle with the U. S. government. He refused to surrender the company to federal control during a World War II labor dispute. President Roosevelt ordered the company seized, and national guard troops physically carried Avery from the building.

An Avery business decision concerning postwar economics is now a classic in business history. Avery had successfully predicted the Great Depression of the 1930's. He was convinced that another and more devastating depression would follow the Second World War. As a consequence, he ordered managers to pull in their belts and canceled expansion plans. While competitors went ahead with aggressive growth plans, Wards sat on reserves of cash and government securities (which eventually totaled more than $325 million) and steadily lost market position, personnel, and momentum.

Ward's wealth tempted Louis F. Wolfson, whose interest was the acquisition of vulnerable companies with sizable liquid assets. In August of 1954, Wolfson launched a now-famous proxy campaign to obtain enough shareholder votes to replace management. A nine-month battle ensued, climaxed by a stormy stockholders' meeting in Chicago on April 22, 1955.

While Wolfson won three of nine seats on the board of directors, he failed to gain control of the company. The fight exhausted Avery, however, and on May 9, 1955, at the age of eighty-one, he resigned. For the next ten years John Barr, the attorney who had guided management's proxy battle to victory, served as chairman.

Although Wards had 568 retail stores in 1955, most of them were in small towns serving rural markets, and not a single new store had been opened since 1941. In 1956 the company spent $8 million to modernize stores with air conditioning, new countertop displays and cash registers, and the installation of catalogue order desks. Unprofitable retail stores were to be replaced by catalogue stores.

Definite proof that Wards had stopped marking time came in 1958 with the opening of the first of a new generation of big suburban shopping center stores in the Lakeside Shopping Center near Denver. This set the pace for other new stores to be located in major metropolitan markets.

John A. Barr

The suburban shopping center became the stage for Ward's retail resurgence, beginning with the opening in 1958 in Denver's Lakeside Shopping Center of its first modern, full-line store since 1941.

Robert E. Brooker

Testing laboratories develop new products as well as monitor the quality of manufacturers' products.

More than two million girls have graduated from Wendy Ward courses which teach social responsibility and citizenship as well as poise and good grooming.

The Turnaround Years

The decade of the sixties is known as the Turnaround Years at Wards. The principal individual who initiated the planning and who motivated the rebuilding of the company into a new, aggressive national retail chain was Robert E. Brooker.

Barr recruited Brooker from his post as president of Whirlpool Corporation to take charge as president of Wards. In addition to his manufacturing experience, Brooker also had fourteen years of merchandising and executive management service with Sears, Roebuck & Co.

One of Brooker's first moves was to assemble a team of executives who were experienced in mass merchandising. This team developed a five-year expansion plan to be financed out of current earnings. The 50 retail stores opened between 1958 and 1961 accounted for an increasing proportion of sales, averaging triple that of the smaller and older stores. The big problem was that about 450 stores still needed to be modernized, replaced, or closed. Another big handicap was Ward's tardiness in entering major metropolitan markets that had been taken over by competitors. It was essential for Wards to develop clusters of stores in these areas.

The mass approach to metro clusters was begun in the San Diego district, where Wards had three stores. They varied in size and stock, acted independently, and all lost money. The three stores were ordered to carry the same goods, thereby enabling them to take part in coordinated advertising and promotion campaigns. The changeover got the stores out of the red in 1963. The San Diego model was next used successfully in the Dallas–Ft. Worth market, combining five stores into a metro cluster. By 1972 Wards was represented by groups of retail stores in twenty-two major metropolitan market areas.

As Wards continued opening new stores and closing old ones, the total number declined, but more merchandise was sold by fewer, larger stores. Sales leaped ahead by almost $200 million in 1964, and the large new metro stores led the way. Modern auto repair, maintenance, and service centers were built with all new stores. Wards also provided heating and plumbing engineering, installation of bathrooms and kitchens, and consultation on interior decorating.

Sources of Ward merchandise constituted a basic problem. Under Brooker the company changed from an "open market" buyer of national brands to a long-term "contract" buyer of private brands, reducing the number of sources in the process from fifteen thousand to seven thousand.

At the Merchandise Research and Development Center in Chicago, technicians in enlarged and newly equipped laboratories analyzed products submitted by suppliers, ran quality checks on production-line merchandise, and made comparative tests of competing products. Keeping the customer firmly in mind, the textile, engineering, and chemistry sections made certain Ward's private brand products, such as Brent, Signature, Riverside, and Hawthorne, performed to advertised specifications. The product design and quality assurance sections guided manufacturers in making products look better and work better.

Advertisements hailed Wards as a family shopping center. Expert guidance on fashions was obtained by setting up a Designer Advisory Council. Designer collections of exclusive apparel were commissioned, assembled, and sent on tour. Ward's fashion coordinators kept a close watch on markets, consulted fashion editors, and advised buyers on the coming styles, colors, and fabrics. A special appeal was made to fashion-conscious teen-agers with the Wendy Ward program, which has taught poise and grooming to several million graduates.

Credit, the service most needed by young homemakers, became more important after 1961 when Wards introduced "Charg-all," its revolving credit plan. Credit sales accounted for an increasing percentage of total sales thereafter.

Development of urban retail markets also stimulated sales by catalogue. By 1963 almost three fourths of catalogue sales were to families living in urban areas. In the good old days, the Wish Book lay beside the family Bible in a farmhouse; in modern, split-level homes it was as handy as the phone book because of the new convenience of telephone ordering. Two general catalogues and numerous special catalogues were distributed each year, a total of 45 million books. (The number was to double in ten years.)

More than 800 catalogue stores were operating in 1964, but the number of retail stores dropped to under 500. In that year 108 catalogue sales agencies, owned and operated by local residents, were established. This was the start of an entrepreneurial program that eventually put more than 1,000 small-town residents into profitable local businesses of their own as representatives of Montgomery Ward.

The bulk and complexity of its transactions swung Wards over to electronic data processing in 1965. At Ward's National Parts Center, established in 1966, computers controlled inventories, shipments, and accounting. Millions of catalogue mailing labels that once took weeks to print were produced by computers in a few days. In 1971 the company completed a network of eleven computerized administrative centers to process both retail and catalogue paperwork.

Several administrative changes took place between 1964 and 1966. After ten years as chairman, Barr embarked on a new career as dean of the Northwestern University School of Management. Brooker served as both president and chief executive officer, and in May, 1966, was elected chairman; Edward S. Donnell became president.

A new corporate symbol—a bright blue rectangle bearing the name in white lettering—was created in 1967 with the consultation of nationally known designers. It identified the new Wards that was to be associated with high quality, fashion leadership, value standards, and above all, customer service.

Ward's sales topped the $2 billion mark in 1969, and its earnings of $43.7 million were the highest in seventeen years. Despite a national economic slump and crippling strikes, volume swelled to $2.2 billion in 1970. Sales approached $2.4 billion in 1971, and the $2.5 billion level was passed before the end of the company's centennial year. Sales

New Ward stores are major retail centers in all-weather regional shopping malls.

Tires, batteries, automotive accessories, and auto repair services are offered by all retail and many catalogue stores.

One of the nation's largest service organizations backs up Ward's guarantees on the products it sells.

Milton Horn, sculptor, puts final touches on bust of Aaron Montgomery Ward. Cast in bronze, it now stands in the Retail Hall of Fame of Chicago's famous Merchandise Mart.

are rising steadily, and expansion is continuing with $75 million to $85 million being invested in new stores and capital improvements annually.

Behind the statistics are many innovations. A test of computerized and modified self-service stores of modular construction in 1969 pointed the way to fast, low-cost construction and lower-cost merchandising techniques. Computerization of merchandise reordering and billing, credit accounts, and financial data also provide new economies and efficiency.

The importance of the catalogue in Ward's world of tomorrow increased as it continued to produce greater sales—almost a quarter of Ward's total sales volume. The future of catalogue merchandising never was brighter. All the means of making sales through the medium of the catalogue are now supported by computer technology. Computers determine the buying trends of 13 million catalogue customers, establish accurate inventory requirements, and automatically replenish them—the objective being to move more goods with proportionately less inventory, yet keep up with rapid changes in consumer wants.

In the past ten years Montgomery Ward has transformed itself from 562 obsolescent, small-town retail stores and a burdensome, manually operated mail-order system into a chain of modern, full-line department stores with 275 new ones in urban areas that account for more than 85 per cent of retail sales and 95 per cent of retail profits.

The post of board chairman lapsed when Brooker retired from the top post in May, 1970. The functions of chief executive officer of Montgomery Ward were assigned to Edward S. Donnell.

Unique and significant recognition of the Ward centennial came when the U. S. Postal Service announced early in 1972 its decision to issue a commemorative stamp to honor the one hundredth anniversary of the founding of the mail-order industry by Aaron Montgomery Ward.

Special recognition also came from Mrs. Virginia Knauer, President Nixon's special assistant for consumer affairs. Speaking before 150 of the country's leading woman's page editors, she said: "Montgomery Ward's one hundred years attest more fully than I ever could to its success in satisfying its customers, and as Wards moves into its second century, it is continuing to provide leadership in searching out and meeting the new demands of consumers."

Today Montgomery Ward is a fast-moving, growing organization committed to the improvement of the life styles of American families. In the words of company president Edward S. Donnell: "The challenges and opportunities of the seventies and beyond are greater than ever for all retailers. Yet, even as we move ahead through the seventies, with all its anticipated improvements in services, we daily reaffirm in millions of individual transactions our one-hundred-year-old credo of 'Satisfaction Guaranteed' as the best of all possible protections for all consumers."

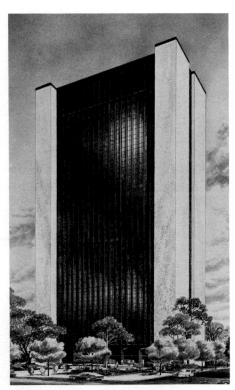

Chicago's first example of the work of world-famous architect Minoru Yamasaki is Ward's new 27-story corporate office building. The cornerstone was laid during the company's centennial year.

14

March 22, 1972

Dear Mr. Donnell:

At a time when our country was first realizing
its great industrial and commercial potential,
mail order retailing meant that the wares of the
city could be shared by our farmers, ranchers
and other rural citizens who otherwise could have
been left out.

Over the years the mail order business has become
an American tradition. It is a tribute to the vision
and pioneering initiative of Aaron Montgomery Ward
that we acknowledge today the significance in the life
of our country of one hundred years of mail order
retailing.

I know that I am joined by grateful men and women
everywhere in memorializing Mr. Ward's achievements and in saluting the continuing growth of the
industry he founded.

Sincerely,

Richard Nixon

Mr. Edward S. Donnell
President and Chief Executive Officer
Montgomery Ward
619 West Chicago Avenue
Chicago, Illinois 60607

The U. S. Postal Service issued this commemorative postage stamp in 1972 to honor the 100th anniversary of the founding of the mail order industry by Aaron Montgomery Ward. The design, by Robert Lambdin, shows a typical rural American family scene late in the 19th century.

American Century

American Century

One Hundred Years of Changing Life Styles in America

Written and Edited by

RALPH K. ANDRIST

AMERICAN HERITAGE PRESS

A DIVISION OF MC GRAW-HILL BOOK COMPANY

NEW YORK   ST. LOUIS   SAN FRANCISCO   DÜSSELDORF

LONDON   MEXICO   SYDNEY   TORONTO

PICTURE EDITOR : *Linda Silvestri Sykes*

ART DIRECTOR : *Jos. Trautwein*

The archives and catalog collections of Montgomery Ward, whose hundredth anniversary was commemorated in 1972, proved to be an invaluable source of material reflecting the changing life styles of our nation's citizens through the past century.

123456789HABP798765432

Library of Congress Cataloging in Publication Data
Andrist, Ralph K.
  American century.

  1. United States—Civilization—1865–1918. 2.
United States—Civilization—1918–1945. 3. United
States—Civilization—1945–   I. Title.
E169.1.A556   917.3'03   72–5533

ISBN 0-07-001795-6

Table of Contents

Introduction

The American Republic, at this writing, has endured for just short of two centuries. It resembles hardly at all the nation created by the Founding Fathers, and changes come faster with each passing year. Once those changes came at a leisurely enough pace so that they could be measured by the generation or decade; today there can be major shifts of direction within the space of months.

This book is an overview of American social life, decade by decade, over the past one hundred years, when the tempo of change has been fastest. In 1872, when this informal history begins, the United States was already embarked on an era of industrialization and technology. Since then it has seen the automobile, the air, and now the space age, each one following more closely on the heels of the last. Each has profoundly affected American ways of life. The family that once took the train to Cape Cod for a month's vacation now has grandchildren who are touring the Far West in a motor home; the frontier town where a sheriff once kept law and order with his fast gun now has uniformed policemen who spend a good part of their time writing out tickets for overtime parking.

As times have changed, people have changed with them. Basically, human nature is undoubtedly what it always was. Love, marriage, birth, and death still arouse the same emotions. But one cannot look at the pictures on some of the following pages without becoming aware that moral standards, for one thing, have changed dramatically over the last few generations. There is a gap wider than the ocean between young Victorian couples on a picnic—carefully and uncomfortably dressed, even to jackets and neckties on the men—and the young men and women at a rock festival in 1970 unabashedly bathing together in the buff in a convenient pond. It may be a new honesty about the human body, or it may be a loosening of moral standards—but either way it certainly is different.

And what of the quality of life—has it improved or deteriorated with the passing years? The immediate answer is that the good old days were always better, for they were the time of our youth, when worries were ephemeral and cares fleeting. We do not, however, all share the same good old days. There are young adults who already look back on the 1950's as the time when there was a golden mist on the earth; there are oldsters whose bittersweet memories are of the years before the First World War. So, while Memory Lane is a pleasant path to follow, it is not a dependable way to reach the truth. Nor will these pages—pictures or text—attempt to say whether life in these United States has changed for the better or worse during the past hundred years. All they will venture is that it has changed—a very great deal.

In this Bicentennial Era of the United States, it seemed timely and appropriate for American Heritage to present a purview of the changing life styles of the people of the United States during its second century—the years that carried us from horse power and the farm to nuclear power and the moon.

R. K. A.

The silk banner above, a souvenir of the Centennial Exposition of 1876, depicts the Arts Building. Opposite, top, is the Corliss steam engine, one of the most popular attractions at the exposition.

The Gilded Age: 1872-79

The 1870's were vigorous if not always genteel. The Civil War was well in the past, and the quarrels over slavery and free soil that had divided the nation for decades were ended. Business was booming; the North was prosperous, and even the ruined South was showing signs of reviving. Railroads were thrusting into new territory; settlers in large numbers were moving into the empty lands of the West. And during the seventies the United States celebrated, with great pride and gratification, its hundredth birthday.

The nation commemorated its first century of existence with a Centennial Exposition in Philadelphia in 1876. Ten years in the planning, it was the biggest thing of its kind ever held in America. There was no midway of rides and fun houses; visitors were content simply to wander among the assembled wonders of science, invention, and the arts. Though fifty countries had exhibits there, the Exposition was mainly a demonstration to the world that the United States had become one of the great industrialized nations. Displayed were farm machines, pocket watches, machine-loomed fabrics, printing presses, mass-produced furniture, incredibly ornate soda-fountain dispensers—all the great and small products of the burgeoning machine age. The ultimate symbol of American technological capability was the huge Corliss steam engine in the center of Machinery Hall, the most powerful engine ever made by man, towering over everything else, quiet, efficient, the prime mover for all the machines in the building.

A sign of the changing status of women in American society was the Women's Building, exhibiting everything from textile machinery tended by young ladies to painting and sculpture by women. A sixty-horsepower steam engine powering the machinery in the building was in the charge of a young woman trained "in theoretical as well as practical engineering." But the biggest attraction was the bust of a girl molded in butter and protected by ice against the hot weather. During

Hoop Skirts and Bustles

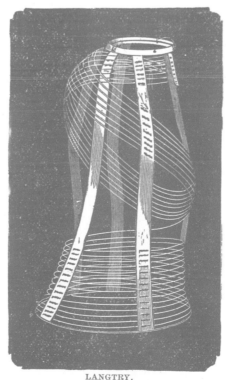

LANGTRY.

4886 Langtry, 27 springs, white hoop skirt and bustle combined.... 90 9 72
The best and most durable Skirt made.

11

HORSE BRUSHES.

Number.		Each.
2676 Horse Brushes, wood back, No. 31....		25
2677 Horse Brushes, wood back, large, No.26		35

2678 Horse Brushes, wood back, Granger, No. 38..... 40

No. 2678.

No. 2679.   No. 2681.

2679 Horse Brushes, leather back, No. 20....... 45   2681 Horse Brushes, sole leather back, No. 83. 90

Misses' Silk Mitts.

No.		Per pair.	Per doz.
314 M Misses' all Silk Mitts, Paris style, made in all new shades, and black................		$0 40	$4 41

Men's Saddles

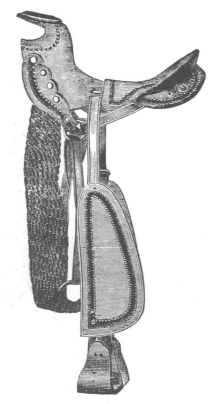

4153 Morgan Tree, half seat, fenders, wood stirrups, hair girth 4 00

the Exposition the sculptress gave a demonstration of her unique art form, and in a burst of virtuosity, using only "paddles, cedar sticks, broom straws and camel's hair [brushes]," she turned two or three tubs of butter into a bust of a "sleeping beauty" in an hour and a quarter.

There were thirty-seven states in the union at the beginning of the 1870's; of these, eleven were west of the Mississippi, and a twelfth—Colorado—would be added before the decade was over, for the open spaces of the West were filling fast. Cities in the East and Middle West were growing tremendously; factories and mills were increasing in number, size, and complexity. The Civil War had forced the creation of large-scale industries for everything from the mass production of uniforms and shoes to the building of ships and the forging of heavy artillery. Industrialization and technology, those two handmaidens of our modern American civilization, were economic and sociologic facts when the war came to an end and the country began to beat its swords into plowshares.

The United States of the seventies, however, was far from being a land of humming factories and sophisticated industry. Much of it was still primitive and rural; there remained extensive regions of dirt roads and isolation, where no communication moved faster than a horse's gallop. The people of the back country were still very provincial, though the war had helped change that. Hundreds of thousands of young men from hardscrabble New Hampshire farms, Louisiana bayous, and Illinois river towns, who otherwise might have grown old on the land where they were born, had marched off to strange places. Once having become aware of a different and exciting world, many were too restless to settle down on the old home place again; some headed for the big cities, while many went to try their fortunes as pioneers and settlers of the West.

Viewed in hindsight, the seventies, despite their energy and bustle, were not the most laudable of years. The moral standards of the times were slack, and there seemed little prospect of a turn for the better, for Ulysses S. Grant was re-elected President in 1872. The smell of corruption had been so strong during Grant's first four years that when he ran again many Republicans joined Democrats in supporting New York *Tribune* editor Horace Greeley. Even so, Grant won easily, because to a host of voters he was still the victorious general in a noble war, whereas Greeley had acquired a reputation as a supporter of far-out causes such as temperance, women's rights, and spiritualism.

Grant was not dishonest, but he was politically naive and undiscriminating in his choice of friends. Given to cronyism, he stubbornly defended those around him even when they were caught in wrongdoing. But it was an era that was complacent about peculations in high places, for the war had left a flabby moral atmosphere, as wars usually do; money was easy despite the recession of 1873; it was a time of expansive enterprises and shadowy deals; and everything had its price, including members of Congress.

But though the easy ethics of the Gilded Age could not help but erode the fabric of the nation somewhat, most citizens were too busy meeting the problems of everyday living to have any time for wheeling and

12

dealing, even if they had had the inclination to do so. For the average person, the style of living was not much different from what it had been before the Civil War. In the cities more homes were lighted by gas, but this was only a change in degree, for illuminating gas had been in use for a long time. Where chimney lamps still flickered—and they did in all villages and on every farmstead—they were almost sure to be fueled by kerosene instead of the once-common whale oil; the young petroleum industry was flourishing, while the American whaling fleet had dwindled and whaling ports like New Bedford had gone into a decline.

At the same time that gas lighting was becoming almost universal in cities in the homes of all but the poor, the gas lamp for street lighting was giving way to a new invention. Philadelphia in 1878 and Cleveland in 1879 became the first cities to replace gas with electric arc lights and were soon followed by other major cities. An even further step into the new world of science and technology was made when Thomas Edison invented the incandescent electric lamp in 1879 and the next year set up a factory for its manufacture, thus opening the way for lighting homes by electricity.

Even in large cities most homes, except for the tenements of slum dwellers, were single-family houses; the day of the apartment house lay ahead. Indoor plumbing was beginning to appear in the United States in the seventies, but as late as 1880 five out of every six Americans had no bathroom at home and either used a public bath or, more likely, bathed in a washtub in the kitchen. The absence of bathrooms meant that the privy was still an essential adjunct to most homes.

There was also a stable behind many city and village homes, for the horse was the only means of private transportation. The typical family used a horse and buggy; a team and carriage indicated a step up the economic scale. Horses also did virtually all the heavy hauling, and city streets often became hopelessly congested with tangles of drays, carts, nervous horses, and cursing teamsters. A pollution problem was created by the quantities of manure that fouled the streets and accumulated in fly-breeding heaps behind thousands of private and livery stables. Some cities gained a little relief with the invention of the cable car, a streetcar propelled by a moving cable in a slot between the rails. The first was installed in 1873 in San Francisco, where the hills were too steep for horsecars; some other cities followed suit. New York took some of the traffic off its crowded streets by building its first elevated railroad. By 1876 forty trains a day were speeding passengers along, making only limited stops and leaving the slow horsecars to those traveling short distances. However, the el created problems of its own, for the trains were drawn by steam locomotives, which belched out soot and cinders and occasionally dropped hot ashes on people below.

The way of life on farms was changing, too, but much more slowly than that of the cities. Though Yankee inventiveness had made farming much more productive and less toilsome over the years with labor-saving devices and machines—the mower, reaper, steel moldboard plow, binder, planter—rural living was much as it had always been. The prime mover on the farm was still animal and human muscle; the

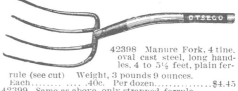

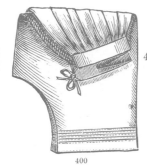

almanac and Bible were read by lamplight; and a farmer's acres came close to being a self-sustaining little kingdom. The dirt roads that connected the farm with the outside world were usually poor in the best of weather, and rain or snow could completely close them for days or weeks. The farm family had to be self-sufficient. The farmer butchered his own hogs, sheep, and cattle, smoked his own ham and bacon and sausage, and usually laid up his own supply of cordwood fuel against the winter. His wife, besides her multitude of housekeeping, cooking, and child-rearing duties, canned and pickled and preserved through the harvest days of late summer and autumn. Thus prepared and provisioned, the family could face winter with equanimity.

The 1870's saw farmers uniting for political action. The Patrons of Husbandry was founded in 1867 as a social organization; by the mid-seventies there were some twenty thousand Granges, or units, with eight hundred thousand members, and the emphasis had changed from social to political. The Granger Movement, as it was called, had become the spearhead of the farmers' revolt against their dependence on outside markets for selling their crops and on the railroads and corporation-owned elevators for hauling and handling them. The Grangers were successful in having legislation passed to regulate warehouse and railroad rates; they also set up many cooperative elevators, creameries, and stores. The movement began to decline after 1876.

A spin-off of the Granger Movement was the mail-order business. The Grangers, in their search for goods at lower prices, became early customers of Aaron Montgomery Ward, who began selling by mail in 1872. Ward's pioneering business probably would have survived without this early Granger patronage, but it did him no harm.

Because of his increasing use of labor-saving machinery, the average farmer was becoming more productive; his marketable surplus above and beyond what he needed for use at home was much greater than his predecessor of an earlier generation had been able to harvest. The first census of the young United States in 1790 showed that nine out of every ten citizens were farm dwellers. In 1870 less than five out of every ten were on farms; a smaller proportion of farmers was needed to feed and clothe the nation. (Another century later, in 1970, there would be less than one person in twenty on farms, so efficient had agriculture become.)

In the West the frontier was no longer marked by forests and log cabins; the line of settlement had moved out onto the treeless prairies and Great Plains, and the new pioneers had to learn to build houses of sod and make fires of buffalo chips because there was no wood. They also found that the plains were a drier land where there was always a danger that drought might wipe out their crops, where prairie fires were a menace, and where all their prospects might be destroyed in an hour by grasshopper swarms that devoured every green plant and even ate clothes left drying on the line.

The rate of settlement of the West was greatly accelerated during the seventies by the railroads and by the legacy of restlessness left by the war. Since 1869, when the golden spike had been driven to join the rails from East and West at Promontory Point in Utah Territory, it had been possible to travel all the way by train to San Francisco or to a good number of intermediate points. Other lines were building; the Missouri Pacific and the Santa Fe were both running trains across Kansas and eastern Colorado to the Rocky Mountains by the mid-seventies, and in the north the Northern Pacific was halfway through Dakota Territory before the chill hand of the recession of 1873 stopped it at the Missouri River for a while. The remote and wild West was becoming much less remote and considerably less wild.

At the beginning of the seventies the Indians and the enormous buffalo herds were obstacles to the advance of the cattleman and the farmer onto the plains. The buffalo problem was soon resolved when a demand for their hides developed. By 1872 the southern plains swarmed with hide hunters who did nothing all day long from early spring till late fall but kill and skin buffaloes. Within seven years the southern herd, conservatively estimated at ten million beasts, had been annihilated. In 1879 the hide men moved into Montana and Dakota territories, and with an expertise born of long practice began blasting away at the millions of animals in the somewhat smaller northern herd. By the end of 1883 only a few dozen forlorn buffaloes remained scattered through all the West.

The Indians did not bow out as unresistingly as the buffaloes. Back in the 1830's, when the Great Plains were called the Great American Desert, the government had promised the red man by solemn treaty that this great grassland would be his forever. It was not long before the white man changed his mind about the value of the plains, and the Indians were forced to cede their lands piece by piece and to move onto ever smaller reservations. The tribes fought to hold their land, until the final epic Indian wars in the seventies, when the United States Cavalry and Indian war parties clashed in scores of engagements from Texas to the Canadian border. The red men were usually defeated, but some of the exceptions were notable in Western annals. None was more spectacular than the annihilation in 1876 of flamboyant, swaggering Colonel George A. Custer, who led half his regiment—225 men—against the Sioux and Cheyenne on the Little Bighorn River, where they were wiped out to a man. But in the long run the tribesmen were doomed by the superior firepower and numbers of their enemies, and by the end of the seventies the Indian wars were over except for a few isolated and tragic incidents.

The cattle frontier followed close on the retreat of the buffalo and the Indian. Steers came up the Chisholm Trail from Texas to meet the new railroads in Kansas; the seventies were the heyday of the cow towns, those points on the railroad where the cattle drives ended and the steers were loaded for shipment east. A cow town was also the place where cowboys, bored and thirsty after a drive that might have lasted many weeks, threw most of a year's wages into a big spree and a monumental hangover. Abilene, Wichita, Hayes, and Dodge City, all in Kansas, and other similar cow towns were wide open within the limits set by the lawmen hired by the law-abiding citizens, and their boot hill cemeteries were in frequent use. The cow town at its height flourished only briefly, the cowboy much longer.

15

WEED "FAMILY FAVORITE."
IMPROVED.

Style 3.—With ornamented machine, black walnut table and cover, drop leaf and two side drawers.
Retail Price, $50.00; Our Price 27.00.

LADIES' POCKET BOOKS.

2783 Morocco, 4 pockets, with specie pocket, silk cord and tassels..... 15

2784 Morocco, 4 pockets, nickel frame, spring lock............. 10

NIGHT LAMP.
MEASURES 7 INCHES TO TOP OF SHADE.

This is a perfect imitation of a stand lamp, all glass, the bases of various colors, and complete in every respect. Price..... 25

Please observe, this Lamp is only 7 inches high. The cut is not a fair representation of its size.

The Centennial Exposition generated tremendous enthusiasm. This contemporary engraving shows

the monumental opening-day traffic jam that developed at Philadelphia's Elm and Belmont avenues.

THE STUMP ON THE MALL

Construction of the Washington Monument was begun in 1848 by a citizens organization, but ten years later the money gave out and work stopped. Mark Twain, with tongue in cheek, described the forlorn stub in the 1870's: ". . . the Monument to the Father of his Country towers out of the mud—sacred soil is the customary term. The skeleton of a decaying scaffold lingers about its summit, and tradition says that the spirit of Washington often comes down and sits on those rafters to enjoy this tribute of respect. . . . The memorial Chimney stands in a quiet pastoral locality that is full of reposeful expression. With a glass you can see the cow-sheds about its base, and contented sheep nibbling pebbles in the desert solitude that surrounds it, and the tired pigs dozing in the holy calm of its protecting shadow. . . ." Happily, the federal government took over the memorial to our first President. Above are the forgotten stump and the vista that became today's Mall, photographed in 1875 from a tower of the Smithsonian Institution.

SOME AMERICAN HOMES

Before the era of standardization, the homes of America were almost as varied as the land itself. At upper left are settlers near Harmon, Colorado; their frame house bespeaks some small degree of affluence, because lumber was expensive in their treeless region. At lower left a Nebraska family poses before its sod shanty with its most valued possessions, including the dining-room table. And above is a family taking the air at its summer residence at Oak Bluffs on Martha's Vineyard. The art of gingerbread architectural decoration reached its full flowering during the seventies.

OVERLEAF: Mrs. E. E. Henry posed, about 1875, for her photographer husband in the living room of their comfortable Leavenworth, Kansas, home. The imposing object behind her is an anthracite baseburner with transparent mica windows, a cheery substitute for central heating.

THE STONES OF
THE TEMPLE

Dwarfed by the huge blocks of stone on which they are working, these men are quarrying granite for the Mormon Temple in Salt Lake City, Utah. The picture was taken in 1872, probably by A. J. Russell. An impressive aspect of the scene is that the workers are going about their task with no evidence of heavy equipment, only sledgehammers, hand drills, and (presumably) explosives to blast the rock apart.

WORKING ON THE RAILROAD

Building railroads, especially in the West, was a major preoccupation of the country for a long time after the Civil War, because settlement and development would have made slow headway without a transportation network. The first route to the West Coast was opened in 1869, when the Central Pacific and the Union Pacific, building toward each other, met at Promontory Point in Utah; at top right, officials of the Central Pacific pose proudly on the great day. The excursion party above is out looking over a portion of the new line and has stopped at a place called Devil's Gate Bridge to have its picture taken. At bottom right, men of the track-laying crew pose with Old Nig, who bears a placard testifying that he hauled up the rails during 750 miles of westward advance of the Northern Pacific.

Between 1875 and 1890 some three hundred so-called bonanza farms, each containing a thousand acres or more, were established in the Red River Valley of Minnesota and North Dakota, a flat, rich region ideally suited for large-scale agriculture. Bonanza

farming was strictly a one-crop system and began to break up in 1890, when crops other than wheat were introduced. Pictured here is a squadron of grain binders at harvest time on the 65,000-acre Grandin farm in North Dakota.

29

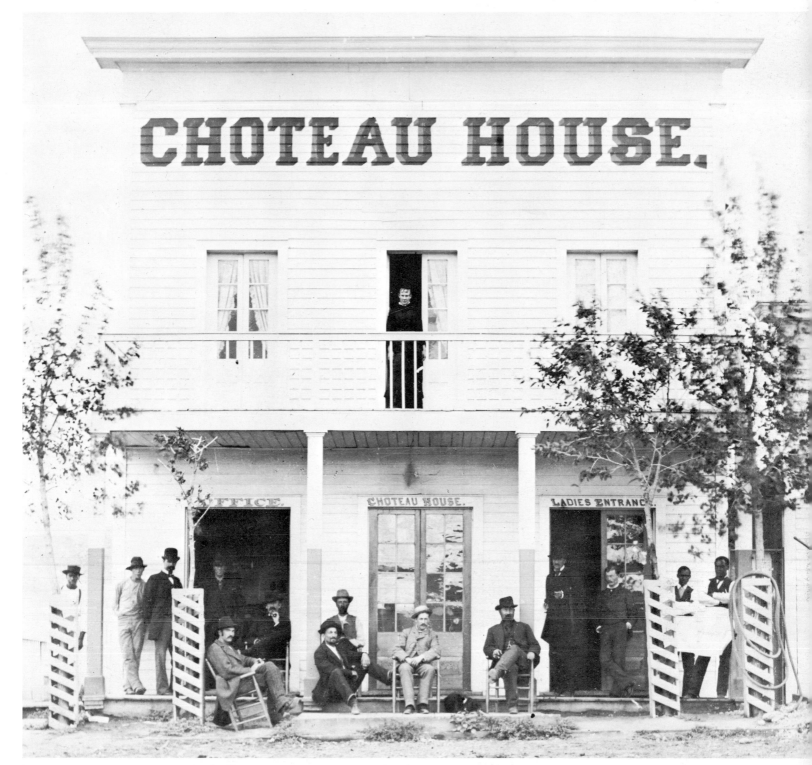

THE WESTERN TRAVELER

Though bad roads and poor accommodations ordinarily made travel in the West during the 1870's an arduous undertaking, they seldom discouraged the stout of heart. The members of the group on the opposite page, identified only as the Brown family, are on their way from Denver to Leadville, Colorado—a trip that will take them, with their small baby, over precarious mountain roads to a mining town at an altitude of ten thousand feet. The Choteau House, above, in Fort Benton, Montana Territory, indicates that amenities were not altogether lacking in the West. The proprietor has thoughtfully provided a ladies' entrance, and contemporary reports were that the hostelry set an excellent table.

THE LOOK OF THE SEVENTIES

Of the coolly self-confident young misses at the left nothing is known except that they were impeccably turned out and came from the vicinity of Cooperstown, New York. All that we know about the bustled beauty above is her name—Mary Stuart. The bustle was in its heyday in the seventies and was "intended to improve the figure, causing the folds of the skirt to hang gracefully."

OVERLEAF: Two women, very probably mother and daughter, pose rather soberly in the front-yard garden of their home. The year is 1878; the city, Denver.

33

"A Mayday at the Central Park Plaza," above, is from an engraving of New York during the 1880's. The belle with parasol in the old circular photograph (opposite page) reigned in the same decade.

In Victorian America: 1880-89

The American citizen of the eighties was just beginning to enter the wonderful world of the appliance and the gadget. Until then the nation's technology had been directed largely toward producing capital goods; it had done marvels in manufacturing locomotives, giant printing presses, steel rolling mills, and farm machinery, but it had hardly entered the home. The telephone came early but modestly: in 1880, only four years after Alexander Graham Bell had patented his device, there were fifty thousand in use; ten years later there were a quarter of a million. Almost all, however, were in places of business; the home phone was still around the corner. The gleam of Thomas Edison's incandescent electric lamp, which he had begun to produce in 1880, was beginning to replace the glow of the gas lamp in many city homes. The first practical phonograph appeared in 1886, and the air has been filled with music ever since. A patent was granted for an electric flatiron in 1882, a step toward freeing women from the tyranny of the sadiron, which required a stove to heat the irons even in the hottest of summer weather.

American medicine and dentistry were well out of the dark ages by the eighties. Anesthesia had long since taken the horror out of surgery, and surgeons were developing procedures that would have been impossible earlier. Yet for all that, the tools of the family doctor when faced with most of the familiar diseases—diphtheria, pneumonia, typhoid—were not much better than they had ever been; he could do little more than try to keep his patient comfortable and hope for a change for the better. The old painting of the doctor keeping his vigil by a child's sickbed as the night hours ticked away may have been sentimentalized, but it was more or less accurate.

HANGING LAMPS.

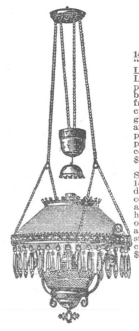

14375 The "Princess" Library Lamp, polished bronze frame, 30 crystal cut glass pendants, complete, with plain white cone shade, $3 48.

Same as No. 14375, with decorated cone shade, and one-half colored pendants instead of all crystal, $3 75.

37

Japanese Parasols.

3300 Job lot Parasols, ladies' size, black and blue, old gold lining, bamboo sticks, each 15c.

3301 Job lot Parasols, ladies' size, bamboo handles, plain shades, light colored sticks, red trimmings, each 15c.

3302 Job lot Parasols, ladies' size, dark colors, old gold. dark sticks and trimmings, bamboo sticks, wound, each 17c,

RAZORS.

46249 Wostenholm's New Pipe, ½-inch finest quality, hollow ground. A little gem, and a dandy shaver: no better steel put in a razor. Every one likes them. Our biggest seller; warranted. Each.................................. $1.00

Gents' Stiff Wool and Fur Hats.

No.   The Morgan.   Each.
5030 Gent's stiff wool Hats, black, similar to cut........................ $1 25

5031 Gent's black stiff fur hats round crown, 2¼ inch brim, 5 inch crown, each $2.00.

5032 Gent's stiff fur Hats, "The Prince," black, crown 5½ in. deep, brim 2 inches, similar to "The Stetson," suitable

The Stetson.

for middle-aged gentlemen, each $2.70.

For those who took care of their own medication, plenty of materials were available. Of all the patent medicines, none had the luster of Lydia E. Pinkham's Vegetable Compound, that boon to womankind. This "Greatest Medical Discovery Since the Dawn of History" was first put on the market by Mrs. Pinkham in 1875 as a sovereign remedy for "female complaints," and by the eighties women were downing unbelievable quantities of it. The compound contained a wide variety of old-fashioned herbs, but an untold number of Victorian ladies would have been shocked to learn that the pleasant glow of well-being they got from a good swig of the compound was caused by the lively 21 per cent alcohol in which those herbs were dissolved. Dr. Hostetter's Bitters, another much-appreciated tonic of the times, contained a jolting 44 per cent alcohol, and in addition was good for a long list of ailments, though for nowhere near as many as Dr. Buckland's Scotch Oats Essence, which modestly claimed that it would "Positively Cure Sleeplessness, Paralysis, Opium Habit, Drunkenness, Hysteria, Neuralgia, Sick Headache, Ovarian Neuralgia, Nervous Exhaustion, St. Vitus Dance, Neurasthenia, &c."

The grocery store of the eighties was still almost a lifetime removed from the principle of self-service. Cookies, crackers, dried apples, sugar, flour, coffee, and other staples arrived in boxes and barrels and were weighed out to order. The same was true of butter, which the grocer ladled out with a wooden paddle, and of kerosene, vinegar, and molasses, which he tapped from a barrel into the customer's own jug. That many of the containers of food sat open, exposed to flies and other contamination, made the old-fashioned grocery a bit less romantic close at hand than it may seem through the mist of retrospect.

The general store is also dear to the hearts of those who view the past with nostalgia. Besides groceries, a general store could be depended upon to supply a horse collar or a corset, a frying pan or a bottle of ink. The store served a purpose in a time of poor communications when every village was a small trading center, but its prices were high and its selections limited. By the early eighties the infant mail-order industry was beginning to give general stores strong competition in the Midwest.

Though the era of moral rigidity and excessive ornamentation known as Victorian lasted for more than a generation, its fullest expression came during the 1880's. The near-mania for overfurnishing homes until there was scarcely space for living did not reach its full flower until the seventies were waning; on the other hand, Victorian prudery and stuffiness began to crumble a small but discernible bit before the high spirits of the Gay Nineties. In the eighties, however, Victorianism was severe and unalloyed.

Queen Victoria was a durable ruler: she ascended the British throne in 1837 and reigned until her death in 1901. However, the era of repression and false modesty to which she gave a name was already well rooted in American behavior before she became queen. Frederick Marryat, a Briton who traveled in this country in the late 1830's, was only one of a number of foreign observers who were struck by the American disposition to call a spade just about anything else. Marryat reported that he offended a young lady who had grazed her shin on a rock by asking if she had hurt her *leg*. On another occasion he entered the reception room of a girls' school to find that the mistress had with great delicacy protected both her young charges and visitors against embarrassment by clothing the four naked limbs of a piano in frilly but proper pantaloons.

That kind of nice-nellyism, one of the many warped offsprings of America's Puritan past, was only a modest presaging of the extremes that were reached in prudish restraints on human relationships by the height of the Victorian age. It was not only that legs were limbs. Body functions ceased to exist, and a young girl of the eighties, after having her first question on such matters answered by an embarrassed mother with the information that the doctor brought babies in his little black bag, often did not exchange another word on the subject with her parent before she was married. Euphemism rose to a fine art. Trousers were "unmentionables" or "unwhisperables" or "nether garments," a chair for some unfathomable reason became a "seat," underpants were mysteriously transmuted into "white sewing," body became "shape." Designations of animals by sex, as "stallion," "bull," "sow," "bitch," and the like, were completely taboo. Yet for some odd reason the explicit term "female" to refer to a woman remained completely acceptable; there were female academies, clubs, boarding schools. Vassar was originally incorporated as Vassar Female College.

The way of a man with a maid was not easy in the smothering red-plush atmosphere of Victorian morality. In 1830 a young man could take his girl sleigh riding or to a dance without her family fearing the worst. Not so in the eighties. The age of chaperons had arrived, for the Victorian mind was not prepared to believe that a boy and a girl, left to themselves, could be trusted to keep their fun always innocent. Wherever they went, or if they remained at home and looked at stereopticon pictures, an eye was always on them. Customs varied with geography, but everywhere Victorian strictures were most rigid among the middle class. Young people had more freedom in rural neighborhoods, while girls in the South were generally watched over with more of an eagle eye than those in the North. Restrictions were for the girls' own good, intoned a writer on etiquette of the time: "Men, as they look back on their own varied experience, are apt to remember with great respect the women who are cold and distant. They love the fruit which hung the highest, the flower which was guarded, and which did not grow under their feet in the highway. . . ."

Surprisingly, in this repressed society there were nearly 29,000 divorces granted in one year of record, 1888. The number is small in a population then close to 60 million, but it was rising every year: in 1878 it had been only 16,000, and by 1898 it would rise to nearly 48,000; divorces were increasing at a rate much more rapid than that of the population. Moreover, two thirds of the divorces granted during that twenty-year period were on the wives' complaints. The increased number of divorces may, as one historian suggests, have been due to the anonymity of city living; that such a large proportion were granted on the wife's complaint possibly indicates that even Victorian women

Children's Silk Hats.

Ages 1 to 6 years. Colors: Navy blue, brown, tan, drab, cardinal, cream.
36574 Child's Silk Hat, shirred brim.
Each..............$0.50
Per dozen........ 5.50

Button Hooks.

8563 All nickel button hooks, 3½ in. long; per doz., 5c.
Per gross.....54c.

8564 Wood Handle Button Hooks,3½
inches long, per dozen..................6c.
Per gross..................................65c.

Patent Saratoga.
Imitation Leather.
LADIES' TRUNK.

Barrel stave top, corners double iron bound, wide hardwood slats, iron bumpers, hasp lock with patent bolt lock on each side, strap hinges, rollers, handles with caps, large tray with bonnet box and parasol case, patent iron stay.
28 inches......... 2 75 | 34 inches........ 3 50

were no longer as servile as their grandmothers and mothers had been. Most divorces were asked on grounds of desertion, though money was said to be the real cause. There were few charges of adultery, possibly because wives accepted the double standard, albeit unwillingly; more likely it was because the parties involved, being Victorians, could not bring themselves to talk about such a thing.

The other facet of Victorian America that so fascinates us, the penchant for overfurnishing and overdecoration, came into prominence during the seventies with the development of machines that could weave carpets, make cut glass, produce furniture, loom printed fabrics, or make almost anything else for the home. Machine-made objects became the rage. Hundreds of thousands of housewives, armed with books on how to decorate in "elevated taste," turned their parlors into jungles of horsehair sofas, ostrich feathers, asparagus ferns, Japanese screens, statues on pedestals, arrangements of dried flowers and milkweed pods, and a hundred other items.

The urge to redecorate reached even into the nation's top address. When Vice President Chester A. Arthur became President on the death of James Garfield, he refused to move into the White House until it had been completely redecorated. Arthur, a widower and a good deal of a dandy, hired as his decorator the famed Louis Comfort Tiffany, who went about his work with great amounts of heavy draperies and buckets of gold paint. The blue of the Blue Room was changed to a robin's-egg shade, and Tiffany's masterpiece, a floor-to-ceiling screen of opalescent glass embellished with "a motif of eagles and flags, interlaced in the Arabian method," was installed in the front hall. To make way for new furnishings, Arthur had twenty-four drayloads of old furniture, among them pieces dating back to early Presidents, hauled out and sold at auction. So much for the aesthetic level of the period.

Though the eighties were intensely Victorian, there was nothing of lavender and old lace about the period. It was an intensely dynamic and acquisitive era. The momentum toward industrialization not only continued but accelerated, spurred by a multitude of inventions and discoveries. These were the years when great commercial and industrial empires were being consolidated: by John D. Rockefeller in petroleum, by Andrew Carnegie in steel and iron, by Philip Armour in meat packing, by many others. At the same time it was not an era dominated by the counting house and the board of directors' table, for the creative ferment was general. American painters and sculptors such as Winslow Homer, Thomas Eakins, and Daniel French were doing some of their best work during the eighties, and a few of the best-selling books published during the decade included Lew Wallace's *Ben-Hur,* Joel Chandler Harris' Uncle Remus books, James Whitcomb Riley's *The Old Swimmin' Hole,* and *Life on the Mississippi* and *Adventures of Huckleberry Finn* by Mark Twain.

However, in a day when money was such an important gauge of success, it was not strange that the favorite reading matter of millions of American boys was the rags-to-riches novels of Horatio Alger, Jr. Although the typical successful American entrepreneur was a self-made man who had built his enterprise by hard work, planning, and initiative, that was not the way Alger's heroes did it. Alger published his first book, *Ragged Dick: or Street Life in New York,* in 1867. Dick was doing no better than anyone else until he rescued a rich man's son who had fallen from a river steamer. The grateful father gave Dick the job that started him up the ladder of success.

Alger continued writing through most of the 1890's, turning out some 120 titles, which sold a reputed twenty million copies. And each book repeated the plot of his first: the hero was getting nowhere until opportunity dropped in his lap, usually as a result of his rescuing a rich man's child from fire, flood, or runaway horse. Alger is considered an apostle of success through hard work. Actually, he told millions of boys that if they waited, the main chance would come to them.

During the eighties the profiles of American cities began to show the first dramatic changes in generations as buildings rose to new heights made practical by the passenger elevator. In Chicago, steel-skeleton construction was used in two office buildings and proved that such techniques were economically feasible in structures more than ten stories tall. In New York the first real luxury apartment building, the Dakota (still a prestige address), was built in 1884 and proved that the wealthy would accept apartment living if it was made comfortable and attractive enough.

Railroad travel, almost the universal way of long-distance inland travel, had grown safer and more comfortable. The Westinghouse air brake, used by most lines by the eighties, had eliminated some of the common causes of accidents. George Pullman's parlor, dining, and sleeping cars were displaying such an exuberance of red plush, stained glass, mahogany paneling, and ornate chandeliers that *The Ladies' Home Journal* complained that they violated good taste—this in a day when overdecoration was the rule!

In the West, the hard winter of 1886–87 brought the great cattle boom to an abrupt end; until then it had been accepted that even on the northern plains cattle could take care of themselves through winter storms. A long series of blizzards reduced large herds to starving remnants, bankrupting even some large cattle outfits. The cattle industry was a long time recovering; things were never the same again, for the open range was gone, and with it much of the Old West.

Though the plains had been settled and the Indians confined to reservations, the West still had its pockets of lawlessness, especially in the Southwest, where mining towns boomed and died. Billy the Kid was slain in New Mexico in 1881 after his brief career of homicide, and Tombstone, Arizona, in the early eighties was the kind of place where Sheriff Wyatt Earp and his henchmen on one side and the Clanton boys on the other could meet in the OK corral and between them kill three men and wound several more in less than a minute. But even then the West was beginning to be a legend, something for tourists to see. Civilization had spread just about across the continent —though a long time would pass before culture would follow everywhere that it had led.

Cherry Stoner.

8849 Cherry Stoners, best known, leave fruit round and plump 65

Ladies' and Misses Sailors.

18378 Seersucker Sailor, in blue and white stripe, cardinal and white, black and white, cashmere band and under brim...................................$0.35

Fly Nets.

No Flies on This Horse.
Cut shows styles of nets quoted as "Body and Breast" nets.
NOTE.—Our quotations for fly nets are not by the pair, but for one single net for one horse.
37490 Upper Leather Team Nets, to head, standard weight, 5 bars, 84 lashes, body and neck. Weight, each net, 3¼ lbs. Each..................$1.85

THE STATUE IN THE HARBOR

The unveiling of the Statue of Liberty was one of the exciting news events of the eighties. A gift from France, it was to have commemorated a century of American independence, but it was not dedicated until 1886, ten years late. Above is the scene as President Grover Cleveland arrives for the dedication. At right an old magazine engraving shows the statue nearing completion in New York Harbor. The torch towers 152 feet above the pedestal, 300 feet above the harbor.

MUSEUM OF THE CITY OF NEW YORK

FUN ON WHEELS

The people on the opposite page are not traveling on a very overcrowded stagecoach: they are vacationers out seeing the sights in a tallyho. The group is composed of Iowans from Sioux City, visiting at Hot Springs, in the foothills of South Dakota's Black Hills, in 1889. The two men above appear to be taking their cycling seriously, and well they might, for they are a long way from the ground. The "safety" bicycle, with two wheels of equal size, first appeared in practical form in 1885, and within five years had almost completely replaced the high-wheelers: the "ordinary," at left, above, and the "star," at right, with small wheel in front.

OVERLEAF: It would be pleasant to believe that this man and woman were also enjoying themselves on wheels, but their expressions suggest otherwise; the lady is giving a photographer a downright hostile look. If they are courting, they appear to find it a joyless pastime.

45

The National POLICE GAZETTE

THE LEADING ILLUSTRATED SPORTING JOURNAL IN AMERICA.

Copyrighted for 1883, by RICHARD K. FOX, PROPRIETOR POLICE GAZETTE PUBLISHING HOUSE, Franklin Square and Dover Street, New York.

RICHARD K. FOX,
Editor and Proprietor.

NEW YORK, SATURDAY, AUGUST 4, 1883.

VOLUME XLII.—No. 30
Price Ten Cents.

A HARLOT'S VENGEANCE.

HOW AN AMERICAN ADVENTURESS GOT EVEN WITH A NOBLE LOVER WHO HAD ALL HE WANTED OF HER, AND GAVE HIM MORE THAN HE HAD ANY USE FOR.

THE DAISIES OF THE DIAMOND FIELD.

HOW THE GIRLS SHAKE THEIR PETTICOATS AND GO IN FOR VIGOROUS AND ATHLETIC EXERCISES WHICH DEVELOP THE MUSCLE, EXPAND THE CHEST, AND KEEP THE BLOOD FROM STAGNATING.

HIGH JINKS AND LOW LIFE

The *Police Gazette* was founded in 1845 mainly as a journal of sporting news, but before long it established its niche in American journalism less as a reporter of sports happenings than as a purveyor of explicitly illustrated stories of crime, sex, and high living. Its illustrators were as skilled as its writers in making much out of little, in showing more of the female figure than the facts warranted (as above), and in embellishing a bit of truth with a great deal of imagination (as in the tale of Yale College revelries at right). It was happiest with a melodramatic tale of illicit love, such as "Harlot's Revenge," opposite, but it could (and did) create a picture story about pillow fights among the girls at Vassar College. The *Police Gazette,* needless to say, was a man's magazine, and its pink cover was always in evidence in the barbershops of the land. It began to fall on lean days when women invaded the barbershops in the 1920's and embarrassed males turned away from their quiet contemplation of its pages. The Depression hastened the demise of the faltering journal, and it expired in 1932.

49

REVELRY RAMPANT.

THE ORGIES INDULGED IN BY YALE STUDENTS AND THEIR FEMALE FRIENDS IN A SUBTERRANEAN CAVE AT NEW HAVEN, CONNECTICUT.

COLLECTION OF DAVID R. PHILLIPS

MANLY LITTLE CHAPS

In 1885 a boys' magazine began printing a serial story called *Little Lord Fauntleroy*. It was an improbable and sugary tale about an American boy who falls heir to an English title and is called to England by an old earl, his grandfather. The first meeting between grandson and earl is described thus: "What the Earl saw was a graceful, childish figure in a black velvet suit, with a lace collar, and with love-locks waving about the handsome, manly little face. . . ." That description and the illustrator's conception of the velvet-suited young lord with his lovelocks affected an army of mothers like a bugle call to action, and for years they made their sons miserable by rigging them out in the same manner. Some of the unfortunate results are shown on these two pages. The authoress, Frances Hodgson Burnett, used her own son Vivian as the model for Fauntleroy; he is the one in the upper right-hand corner of this page.

SETTLING THE WEST

Although the pioneering days were fading into the past over much of the West during the 1880's, the Chrisman sisters (above), daughters of a Nebraska rancher, were having their own go at pioneering when their picture was taken. They had each taken a 160-acre homestead claim, and two or more took turns living together in sequence on the four claims to satisfy land-office residence requirements. Frontier days were long past at the farm near Moro, Oregon (right), where the wheat harvest is under way. Thirty-two horses pull the combine harvester under the command of a driver who perches on a thronelike seat. As for Garden City, in western Kansas (top, right), this picture shows that it was not only settled but also up-to-date in 1887, for it had its own horsecar. Its route was short—from the prairie at one end of the main street to the prairie at the other.

AT THE WATERFRONT

Seaports have always fascinated the landlubber. They have a special smell, a sense of coming from and going to far places, and a different breed of men. On the opposite page is a wharf at the South Street seaport in lower Manhattan; although small steam craft can be seen here and there, sailing ships still completely dominated the open oceans during the eighties. The building above, on the San Francisco waterfront, had seen better days but was still the center of a good amount of rowdy activity. Built in 1856, Warner's Cobweb Palace was enormously popular with seamen, but by 1880 it had fallen into this sad state of decrepitude. The boys and girls in the photograph were not habitués of the dive but merely curious passers-by.

In 1888 photographer Leonard Dakin set up his tripod to get this view of the village of Cherry Valley,

New York, and a party enjoying the day. Cherry Valley remains, not larger but changed by time.

A COTTAGE FOR THE SUMMER

For generations of Americans, summer vacations have meant a cottage or cabin somewhere by the water, whether mountain lake, river, or ocean. But family resources vary, and one man's cottage might be someone else's mansion. The summer house above on the Massachusetts coast might be taken for one of many that stand today on the same seashore except for the 1880's costume worn by the lady with the book and the ladder-back chairs outside. Also, the two ladies on the rock in the background protecting themselves from the sun with umbrellas would today be in bikinis under the open sky. The group opposite is posing in 1887 on the steps of the Newport, Rhode Island, "cottage" of socialite Stewart Brice Bennett. Newport was then the summer playground of the very rich, and some of its "cottages" were brick and marble architectural fantasies with dozens of rooms. Mr. Bennett's cottage appears a rather modest one by Newport standards of the times.

SYRACUSE UNIVERSITY PRESS

The bit of strenuous action above refutes the belief that all young Victorian ladies were wan, wispy, and forever fainting. The scene is near Cherry Valley, or Waldron, New York; the time, August, 1888. Below are three robust Victorian females—with escort—from the other side of the country; they are picnicking and fishing near Jacksonville, Oregon. The three pretty girls on the opposite page were photographed in New York City in 1889.

JACKSONVILLE MUSEUM, JACKSONVILLE, OREGON

OVERLEAF: Nothing was more pleasant than to gather around the piano and sing. These young people were photographed in Upland, New York.

Some childhood games change with time; the best are ageless. William S. Mount's drawing of a bubble-blowing girl shows one child's favorite pastime. Winslow Homer sketches an old, old diversion (right).

Pleasures and Pastimes

Like many other activities when America was a little younger, games and amusements were simpler and far less expensive than they are today. People made their fun with whatever was at hand: a frozen millpond, a hay-filled bobsled, a fiddle and a barn floor, an ocean beach when the signs were right for a clambake, a thicket of ripe plums that inspired a combined picnic and fruit-gathering expedition. Except in cities there was little for the person who preferred to be a spectator to do; in country and village the choice between joining in the fun or staying home was usually clear-cut.

Children, too, were on their own. No one had heard of supervised play; no one conceived of dressing small boys like miniature professional baseball players and egging them on to fulfill their fathers' youthful dreams of glory. When boys played ball, they gathered in a pasture far from a parental presence and chose up sides for a game of one old cat. Childhood play was made up of ingenuity and some age-old ingredients: the swing, the raft, the swimming hole, the tree house, secret woodland nooks. There was a wealth of games: follow-the-leader, prisoners' base, hopscotch, king-of-the-mountain, hide-and-seek, which was best in long summer twilights, and fox and geese, for days when new-fallen snow covered the ground. Two boys with a pocket knife could pass the time happily absorbed in the intricacies of mumblety-peg; and for a boy or a girl alone on a summer afternoon there was always sun-warmed grass to lie on, slow-moving clouds overhead to contemplate, and the secret thoughts of childhood for company.

William Mount's "Dancing on the Barn Floor" depicts a rural version of a universal recreation. In Winslow Homer's "Gathering Berries" (below), what could be a chore becomes a social occasion.

Eastman Johnson's "The Old Stagecoach" (above) gives a view into a child's world of make-believe. "Sugaring Party" (below), also by Johnson, shows the long-ago sociability of maple-sugaring time.

OVERLEAF: Skaters of the 1870's throng New York's Central Park, then still being landscaped.

OLD PRINT SHOP

The quiet pleasures of music are explicit in Thomas Eakins' "Home Ranch," painted in 1890.

When Edward Lamson Henry painted "News Office" (above) he may have had something different in mind, but he was pointing out a favorite human pastime, gossip: not malicious tale-telling, but sincere interest in one's neighbors. Winslow Homer's "Crack the Whip" (below) pictures a boys' sport once known to every playground.

The elegantly furnished Hoffman House bar was a favorite meeting place for New York's young men about town during the nineties and was renowned for its lavish display of buxom nudes.

The Gay Nineties: 1890-99

The 1890's may have more of a reputation for gaiety than they deserve, for the decade was not all beer gardens and German bands, strawberry festivals, and bicycles built for two. Many Americans were working too hard and were too short of money to share in the fun; indeed, there were some who were having a rather gloomy time of it. Even so it was a bustling, energetic, exuberant era, full of so much high spirits that "Gay Nineties" is as descriptive a label as any.

It was not only light hearts and laughter that made the nineties memorable; it was not just that—at least in memory's rosy afterglow —the barbershop quartets sang in exquisite harmony and the girls were achingly lovely in their shirtwaist dresses and pompadoured hair. For besides their reputation as a carefree decade, the nineties were a watershed period in American history, a time when the nation turned its back on many old ways and set out on new courses.

An early indication that an old order was passing came in an announcement by the superintendent of the census saying that according to the 1890 census the frontier was gone: "At present the unsettled area has been so broken into isolated bodies of settlement that there can hardly be said to be a frontier line." Ever since the white man had first landed on the Atlantic shore there had been a western frontier as an outlet for the energies of an expanding people, a place where a man who had failed in the East could go for a new start, a land where those so inclined could find adventure. With the frontier gone there would be profound adjustments in the dynamics of American life.

Another remarkable change during the decade was a dramatic shift in the origins of new Americans. From the beginning the immigrants who peopled the American republic had come—except for those dragged unwilling in chains from Africa—almost entirely from north-

73

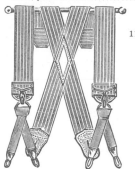
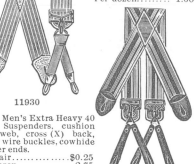

ern Europe: the British Isles, Germany, Scandinavia. Then the main source shifted, and during the nineties and later the ships brought from southern and eastern Europe a tide of alien peoples speaking strange tongues: Serbs, Greeks, Bulgarians, Italians, Russian Jews. Most of them found jobs in cities or became coal miners or steelworkers. Native-born Americans shook their heads at the invasion, but the United States had become the Great Melting Pot. It was no longer necessary to be Anglo-Saxon or Nordic to become an American.

Though the national conscience no longer tolerated the unabashed freebooting of former years, there were many opportunities for a shrewd man to become wealthy—and to be rich was to be an admired and honored personage. Even churchmen made their bargain with money. Bishop William Lawrence of Massachusetts proclaimed that "Godliness is in league with riches," and the Reverend Russell Conwell, rector of Philadelphia's Grace Baptist Church, repeated across the country some three thousand times his "Acres of Diamonds" lecture with its exhortation to the audience, "I say, get rich, get rich! But get money honestly or it will be a withering curse." Only the lazy, said Conwell, shrank from the stern duty of laying up riches.

Despite Conwell's warning that dishonest money would be a curse, many men risked damnation. However, commercial success was not necessarily achieved by fleecing the public. Frank W. Woolworth, for one, expanding his chain of red-and-gold-fronted stores, needed no chicanery to induce customers to buy articles of good quality never before seen at his prices of five and ten cents. And Aaron Montgomery Ward with his mail-order catalogues was not only freeing the back country from dependence on the local general store with its limited and expensive stock, but was making a pledge unheard of in a day of *caveat emptor*—"satisfaction guaranteed or your money back."

There were by the early nineties almost forty-five hundred millionaires in the country, and many of them were flaunting their fortunes very ostentatiously. In New York enormously costly houses furnished in extravagant magnificence went up along Fifth Avenue, and the same men who built them put up "cottages" at Newport, Rhode Island; these pretentious structures in a conglomerate of architectural styles, boasting dozens of rooms and manned by small armies of servants, were meant to be occupied only a few weeks of the year. Every city of any size had its section where the very wealthy congregated and built their ornate residences: Nob Hill in San Francisco, Chicago's lake front, Summit Avenue in St. Paul, and many others. These were the times of private steam yachts with crews of fifty, of private railroad cars, of costume balls that cost well over a hundred thousand dollars. If nothing else, the new-rich put on a glittering spectacle.

Unfortunately, the same industrialization that was creating more rich men than ever before was also bringing about more poverty. Many jobs were at the whim of the machine; when the factory went idle, the worker and his family suffered. City slums grew bigger, if not uglier. And because it was still a day of stern individualism and the Puritan ethic, the plight of the wretched was considered to be of their own making and its remedy their responsibility alone.

The day of the independent artisan was drawing to a close. The small-town blacksmith, the journeyman carpenter, the independent mason, were still far from extinction, but many other craftsmen had become factory workers, their skills diluted in mass production piece-work. By 1898 more than seventeen million Americans out of a total population of about seventy-five million worked in factories. That one statistic said a great deal more about the times than did all the lyrics of barbershop harmony.

Farmers, especially in the South and Midwest, were another group that had little to be lighthearted about during the nineties. Times had been bad for them since the mid-eighties; most of them barely managed to make ends meet, all the while damning the banks that collected interest on their mortgages and the railroads that charged higher and higher rates to haul their harvests. When the depression of 1893 came, tens of thousands of them lost everything. They sought their messiah in thirty-six-year-old William Jennings Bryan, who stampeded the Democratic convention in 1896 with his "Cross of Gold" speech. But Bryan lost to William McKinley, who believed in the gold standard, sound money, and a high tariff.

City skylines changed dramatically during the nineties as architects and engineers mastered the steel-skeleton method of construction. New tall buildings rose not only for office use but also for apartment living. The move into apartment buildings meant abrupt wrenches from traditional living styles; gone were the shaded yard, the front porch, even the front parlor, which just did not fit into apartment-building architecture.

As cities grew upward they also spread outward, giving birth to satellite communities spawned by the railroads and the electric trolley. The first practical electric streetcar began operating in Richmond, Virginia, in 1888; in 1890 there were scarcely more than a thousand miles of electric trolley track in all the country, but before the nineties were over the clanging of the streetcar's bell was heard not only on city streets but far beyond the city limits.

The traditional isolation of rural life was greatly eased in 1896 with the inauguration of rural free delivery. Among other things it brought the daily newspaper to the back roads, giving the farmer current market information and making him as aware as his city cousin of events in the outside world. When parcel post was also added to the postal services in 1913, the farmer could get all but his bulkier mail-order purchases delivered right to his mailbox, and the semiannual catalogue assumed an even more important place in country living.

In 1890 there were a quarter of a million telephones hanging on walls; ten years later there were three times as many, and wires were being feverishly stretched to keep up with the demand for more. The technical quality of the telephone also improved during those ten years, but it still required an attentive ear and was not yet ready for those interminable, intimate woman-to-woman conversations.

The safety bicycle, with two wheels of equal size, had almost entirely replaced the "ordinary," with its large front wheel and small rear wheel, by the beginning of the nineties. The pneumatic rubber tire

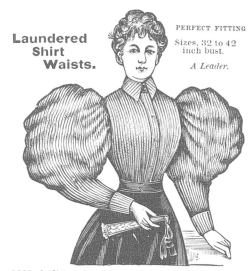

Laundered Shirt Waists.

PERFECT FITTING
Sizes, 32 to 42 inch bust.

A Leader.

5820 Ladies' Shirt Waists, made of light chambray prints; in pink, blue, heliotrope, gray or tan stripes or figures, also checks in pink, blue or gray, stiff laundered collar and cuffs, plain belt, all felled French seams, pointed shirt yoke in back. Each........$0.48 Per dozen..... .... 5.60

Sleeve Protectors.

Per pair. Per doz.
11810 Men's Good Print Oversleeves, patent rubber top $0.10 $1.00

Cook's Windsor for Wood.

Cook's Windsor, for wood only, has a door on each end of fire box, nickel ornaments, ground edges, large fire box, patent oven door opener, towel rod, heavy false bottom in fire box, a swing fender and outside nickel oven shelf.
44090 Plain Square, without reservoir, for wood only.

Size.	Oven.	Fire box.	Weight.	Price.
8-20	18x21x12	24x10 in.	275 lbs.	$14.00
9-20	20x21x12	24x10 "	275 "	14.58
8-22	20x22x12	26x11 "	300 "	16.20
9-22	22x23x12	26x11 "	300 "	16.75

Black Boards.

Double Breasted Square Cut Sack Suits.

was introduced in 1889 and was almost universal within two or three years; the safety bicycle and air-filled tires together put the nineties on wheels. Cycling clubs proliferated. On Sundays many avenues were filled curb to curb with earnest cyclists enjoying fresh air, exercise, and good fellowship. The sport was open to women as well as men, and though conservatives clucked about the display of calf on the downstroke, they were fighting a losing battle, for the young lady of the time was freeing herself from some ancient shackles and would show considerably more limb before she gained her point.

The typewriter contributed a great deal more to the freeing of women than did the bicycle. A practical typewriter had been on the market since the 1870's, but the maker had tried, with little success, to sell it as an aid to writers and ministers. Around the beginning of the nineties the thrust of promotion was changed to feature the usefulness of the machine in business, and it was soon discovered that a woman could not only type as fast as or faster than a man and as accurately but— more important—do it for less money. The result was inevitable. By 1900, 206 out of every thousand girls older than sixteen were employed as office workers; for the first time a career besides marriage was open to hundreds of thousands of young women.

The young lady of the nineties, working or not, developed a style and manner unique to her time, so that even in an old photograph she is identifiable as belonging to her decade. That look was in large part the creation of illustrator Charles Dana Gibson. Undoubtedly the Gibson girl appealed to women because that splendid creature of ink and paper typified what most of them yearned after: beauty, self-assurance, freedom from the old subserviency of woman to man while retaining the power to win a man or to scorn him as whim or occasion dictated. Her hair was piled up in a magnificent pompadour, and she wore a crisp shirtwaist and a long skirt. Her stride was free, and she played such games as tennis and golf not mincingly but with gusto. It was not surprising that women tried to imitate her, if not always with complete success.

A good gauge of the temper of a people is the celebrities they admire —and during the nineties they took a lively interest in some rakish types. There was, for one, Diamond Jim Brady, so called for his two-million-dollar collection of gems though his main interest in life was eating. A typical dinner might see him put away two or three dozen large oysters, half a dozen crabs, double portions of soup and terrapin, a brace of wild ducks, a large steak, and all the trimmings, including a variety of desserts. Diamond Jim's other love was comic opera star Lillian Russell, fair of face and well rounded of form, who had a fine voice but was a little scant on acting ability. Lillian never consented to marry Jim—he remained single all his life—but she was true to him in her way through four marriages.

John L. Sullivan was the last of the bare-knuckle champions, and even after he had done most of his training on booze his pile-driver fists did not fail him until he met Gentleman Jim Corbett in 1892 in the first championship fight with gloves. Sullivan not only lost the championship but ended a budding career on the stage (he had played

Simon Legree in *Uncle Tom's Cabin* and had starred in a play written especially for him, *Honest Hearts and Willing Hands*); he retired to saloonkeeping. Gentleman Jim had his fling at acting, and when he lost to Bob Fitzsimmons in 1897, Fitz in turn went on the stage. His vehicle was called *The Honest Blacksmith*, for Fitzsimmons had once been a smith, and during the big scene he clanged away at an anvil, actually shaping horseshoes. There were competent actors during those years, but the popularity of pugilists on the stage was a tidemark of the general level of the performing arts of the time.

A people's songs are another barometer of their emotional climate, and the nineties were singing years. The melodies tended to be uncomplicated and the lyrics either boisterous or unabashedly sentimental, but they were eminently singable. "A Bicycle Built for Two" was virtually the theme song of the nineties. Many songs carried a moral, usually that it was better for a girl to be pure but ragged than to sell her virtue for gold: "She Is Only a Bird in a Gilded Cage," "She Was Happy Till She Met You," "She Is More to Be Pitied than Censured." And there were a good number of rollicking tunes, perfect for singing in beer gardens: "The Man on the Flying Trapeze," "There Is a Tavern in the Town," "The Bowery." When "The Sidewalks of New York" was first played in 1894, the audience was so captivated that it sang the chorus along with the star; today the song is almost the city's anthem.

The shadows began to fall on this carefree time with the Spanish-American War. America went into the conflict as it had done everything else during the nineties, with wild enthusiasm. The war was won at remarkably low battlefield cost to the United States—only some 385 killed—but as a result of miserably neglected sanitation and putrid food, fourteen men died of disease for every one killed by a Spanish bullet. Lesser mismanagements included such things as sending troops into the tropics in woolen winter uniforms. The lasting effect of the war was to make the United States a colonial nation, with obligations that remained long after the bands stopped playing. For good or bad, the nation left the Gay Nineties and entered the twentieth century with the headaches of imperialism and a commitment in Asia from which it has been unable to extricate itself.

One other development of the nineties was to have a profound effect on generations yet unborn, on the very shaping of cities and countryside. By the mid-nineties a number of men were experimenting with self-propelled contraptions designed to travel on the public roads, and in the spring of 1898 the first automobile built in America for the market was sold. Two years later eight thousand horseless carriages were registered. Most coughed and snorted and emitted gas fumes as they moved about; some hissed and put out puffs of steam; here and there a few electrics glided along as silently as ghosts. The age of the automobile was at its threshold, and Daisy Bell would not much longer be satisfied to share a bicycle built for two.

The Banner Mammoth Lamp.
400 Candle Power Light.
55692 The Mammoth Lamp gives a strong and brilliant light, and has a fount holding one gallon of oil; it is the only mammoth lamp with extra wick feeder to supply oil to the burning wick; suitable for all places where a large and steady light is required; 20 inch embossed tin shade harp, smoke bell and chimney; ready for use.
Price $3.25

Manure Hooks.

42403 Manure Hooks; weight, 3½ pounds.
Each $0.35
Per dozen............................3.90

Polished Brass Cuspidors.
45218 Cuspidor, polished brass, not nickel plated; has oxidized ornamental band around base; a very handsome pattern; is full size.
Each.................................$0.60
Per dozen............................6.48

Bath Tubs.

45205—Infants' Bath Tub; weight, 10 to 25 lbs; japanned tin. Size
27 inch $0.95
30 inch 1.05
33 inch 1.25
36 inch 1.45

IN A VICTORIAN PARLOR

The Victorian parlor was a place meant for things, not people. The clutter above is identified as Mrs. Leoni's parlor, the place is New York City, and the time of year is apparently the Christmas season, to judge by the wreath in the window and the greenery on the overhead gas lamp. A piano was regarded as a treasure and a luxury, since at that time if you wanted music you had to make it yourself; later the phonograph enabled the untalented to share in the delights of good music. The peaceful scene opposite is from Portland, Oregon, about 1895. The knitter, Mrs. J. G. Robbins, was photographed by her sister, Mrs. Lee Hoffman, in Mrs. Hoffman's front parlor.

COLLECTION OF MARGERY HOFFMAN SMITH

CONCERNING COUNTRY ROADS

At the close of the 1890's, when the picture opposite was made near Media, Pennsylvania, horses and wagons could still travel peacefully on country roads in America. When the automobile arrived, such scenes soon disappeared. Above is a picture that speaks for itself: a big wood-burning range and a good cook were essentials in every home.

An elementary school class in Washington, D.C., receives a lesson in the methods of commerce from the iceman, who is here demonstrating how a block of ice is weighed. When it is over there will probably be a piece of ice for each child to suck on, a treat few remember today.

OVERLEAF: *In a nation still overwhelmingly rural the one-room country schoolhouse remained the backbone of American education in the 1890's. This one could have been almost anywhere, so alike in appearance were such schools, but it was, in fact, located in Maine.*

THE GIBSON GIRL

Though Charles Dana Gibson continued to draw his lovely and captivating Gibson girl into the early 1900's, her zenith was the Gay Nineties, and to mention one is to evoke the other. In creating this vital creature after whom millions of young American women tried to pattern themselves, Gibson struck an early blow for female liberation. For his girl the swoonings and vapors of the Victorian maid were passé; she needed freedom to walk and bicycle, and she got it by loosening her clothes. Though she still looks rather nipped in by today's standards, she was much freer than the tightly constricted women of preceding decades. There was also a Gibson man, but he was so impossibly handsome that no male of the period ever seriously tried to imitate him.

FORE!

THE AMERICAN GIRL TO ALL THE WORLD

THOSE NAUGHTY GIRLS

The Gay Nineties have a reputation for naughtiness that may be more hearsay than fact. It was probably acquired because in those Victorian days any show of high spirits was likely to be considered indiscreet. The languid lady at far left on the opposite page is Anna Held, a singer brought from France in 1896 by producer Florenz Ziegfeld, who gave her instant stardom by announcing in the press that she bathed in milk every day. The other lady opposite is Little Egypt, who introduced a great many men at Coney Island to the Oriental belly dance; although it first appeared in the United States at the Algerian Village of the Columbian Exposition of 1893 in Chicago, Little Egypt took the art to Coney Island. As for the 1898 bathers above, their *ta-ra-ra-boom-der-e* pose seems a bit indelicate. The nineties were clearly not lacking in press agentry and showmanship.

89

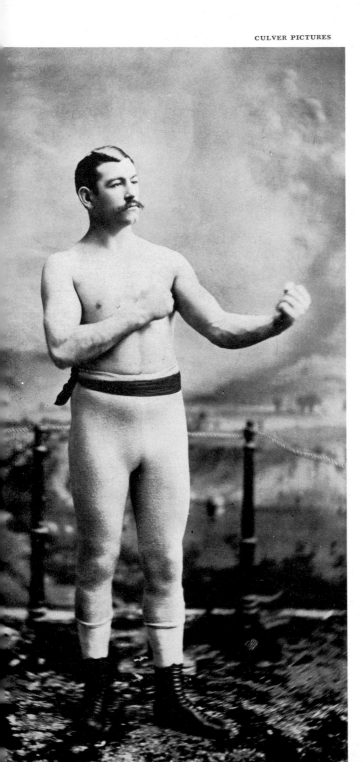

THREE CELEBRITIES

The nineties, like every other period, had its special celebrities and heroes. John L. Sullivan (at left), a great fighter and drinker, was heavyweight champion until 1892. This photograph is of a somewhat younger Sullivan. The man above in the derby hat is Diamond Jim Brady, renowned for his wealth but even more for his gargantuan appetite. On the opposite page is Lillian Russell, an Iowa girl who made it big in musical comedy on Broadway. She and Jim Brady were close friends, but though she found time for four husbands, she never married Jim.

90

COPYRIGHT 1893
BY
W. M. MORRISON.
CHICAGO.
26

GROUP PORTRAIT

If there is any of the ham actor in a person, a camera will usually bring it out—and that was apparently as true in the 1890's as it is today. When photographer Harry Putney posed the clientele of a Leavenworth, Kansas, beer parlor in front of their saloon, the older men in back took the occasion seriously, but the young sports in front could not resist burlesquing the role of tosspots. The young man at the extreme right, as his contribution, has carried from the bar an advertisement showing a young lady enjoying her glass of beer.

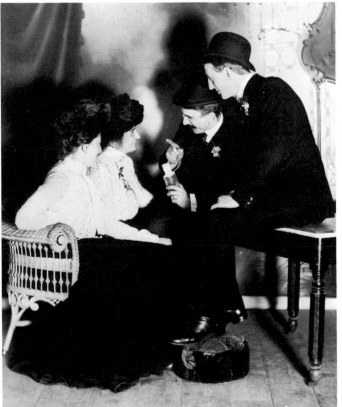

TWO BY TWO

The nineties had no more of a monopoly on romance than any other period, but the decade was very sentimental about the subject and produced many songs about love, both unrequited and requited. The couple above are exchanging the usual sweet nothings on Midland Beach in New York in 1898. Chansonetta Emmons, who left a priceless photographic record of life in her native Maine, made the picture of the two young hand-holders (opposite, top). And on the opposite page, bottom, the two young blades appear to be trying to fast-talk the ladies into something; the latter seem to be enjoying it.

95

Horse racing is still with us, but the nineties were the last years when it was the only kind of racing. The harness racers above are pounding around the Leavenworth, Kansas, racetrack (now

Shrine Park) in some long-forgotten race in 1895. After the turn of the century the automobile, and the motorcycle as well, began roaring around raceways and the tracks at county fairs.

SUMMERTIME

The Gay Nineties had quiet moments, among them tranquil summer days in unspoiled countrysides that are now gone forever. On the opposite page, top, a family group, complete with banjo duo, takes its rest during a decorous outing somewhere in New England. Opposite, bottom, staff and guests pose on the grounds and verandas of the Spray View House at Ocean Grove, New Jersey. Once such scrollwork inns abounded from oceanside to mountains; now all but a few museum pieces have given way to modern buildings. The photograph above tells its own story; the girls are wading in Baird's Creek in Wisconsin.

One of life's pleasures in the nineties was riding through a summer countryside in an open trolley.

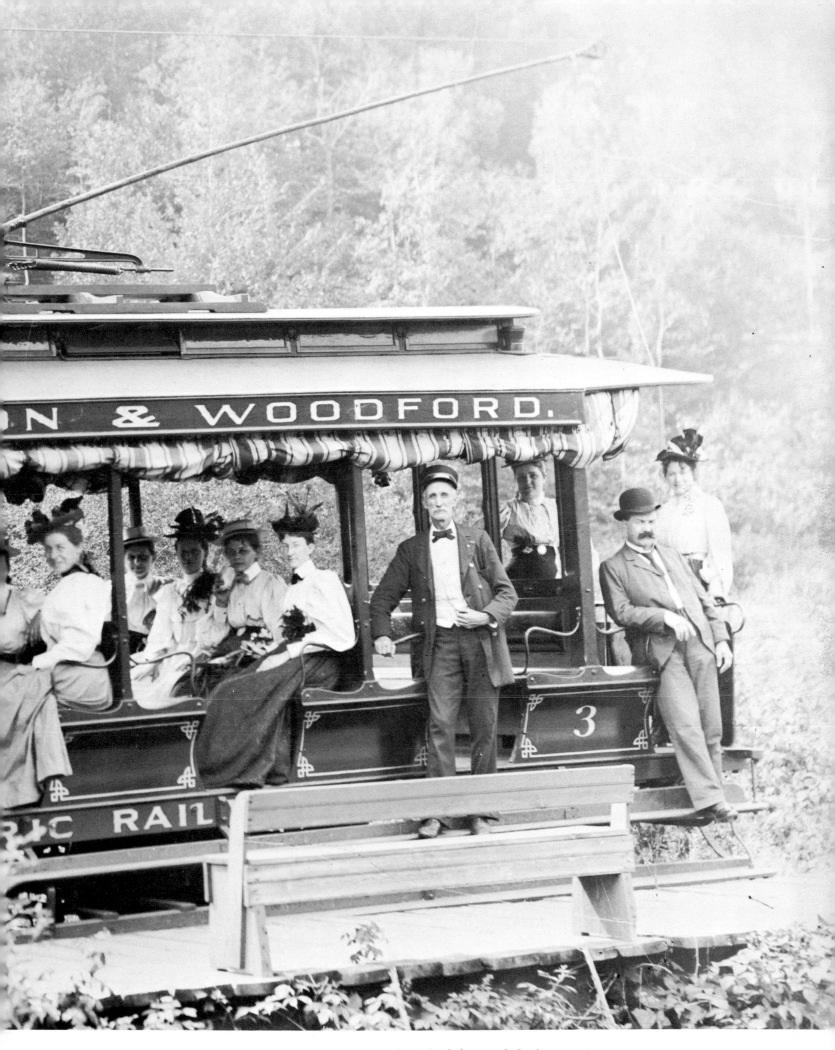

This one ran from Bennington, Vermont, to an amusement park. A flood destroyed the line in 1898.

At noon on August 16, 1893, the government opened to settlement six million acres of the Cherokee Outlet, with this frantic melee. Long before nightfall claims had been staked out over the en-

tire huge area, and hundreds of tents dotted the prairie. The Outlet, which had once been guaranteed in perpetuity to the Cherokee Indians, was made a part of the Territory of Oklahoma.

William T. Smedley's wash drawing of the beach at Narragansett Pier, Rhode Island, in 1900 evokes turn-of-the-century America. The two ladies at top right pose with a 1909 model electric runabout.

Into the Twentieth Century: 1900-1909

The arrival of the year 1900 brought an outpouring of editorials, sermons, and solemn punditry about the achievements of the past century and the challenge of the one ahead. Chauncey Depew, former railroad president and at that moment a junior United States senator, looked on the times and found them good: "There is not a man here who does not feel 400 per cent bigger in 1900 than he did in 1896, bigger intellectually, bigger hopefully, bigger patriotically, bigger in the breast from the fact that he is a citizen of a country that has become a world power for peace, for civilization and for the expansion of its industries and the products of its labor." Senator Depew's syntax was slightly murky and his rhetoric a bit turgid, but his meaning was clear. The Reverend Newell D. Hillis, pastor of Brooklyn's Plymouth Church, saw America through glasses even rosier than Depew's: "Laws are becoming more just, rulers humane, music is becoming sweeter and books wiser; homes are happier, and the individual heart becoming at once more just and more gentle."

There were many predictions of what the twentieth century would bring forth. The Englishman H. G. Wells, who had something of a reputation as a seer, ventured a look at the United States of the future and correctly forecast the growth of megalopolis in the Northeast, the development of divided-traffic, limited-access highways, the electric dishwasher, the freight-carrying motor truck and the passenger bus, and many other inventions. Sometimes he missed, and sometimes his timing was merely off, as when he thought that "long before the year 2000 A.D., probably before 1950, a successful aeroplane will have soared and come home safe and sound." Another writer, who now appears to have little chance of making good on his prediction,

105

Blizzard Ice Cream Freezer.

This is a single action Freezer. The can revolves, while the beater remains stationary, and we claim for it that it will do its work as well as any other freezer in the market. The can to this freezer may be revolved after the beater has been removed,which is a decided advantage in freezing fruits. The tub is strong. Cans are made from charcoal tin plate, tinned beater with double self-adjusting wood scraping bar. It is positively the best freezer in the market for its cost.

C 5905—

Size, qts.	2	3	4	6	8	10
Weight, lb....	8¾	10½	12¾	17	21¼	29
Each.........	$1.38	$1.53	$1.79	$2.33	$2.92	$3.97

This freezer is not made larger than 10 qts.

Feather Dusters.

13640 Body Feather Duster, 8-inch handle and 6-inch feathers.
Each $0.10
Per dozen.................... 1.00
Weight, 6 ounces.

13642 Body Dusters, full and soft, 10-inch handle and 7-inch feathers.
Each..........$0.15
Per dozen.... . 1.65
Weight, 8 ounces.

The woven down duster, flat, not round,has no equal; double faced soft, downy wiper that gathers up the dust and when filled with dust can be taken from the room and beaten out in a moment.

Decorated Vase Lamps.

B 1359 Extra Large Parlor, Reception or Table Lamp, height to top of chimney 32 in., diameter of bowl and globe 12 in. The oil pot is solid brass, gold plated, as well as the feet and the crown trimmings. The decorations are done by hand and consist of white, pink and red chrysanthemums arranged in large clusters with natural foliage on a back ground of cerise, shading to pink; also decorated with American Beauty full blown roses and buds with leaves and stems in their natural colors on a back ground of imperial green, shading to ecru at center. This is the style and size lamp usually sold by retail dealers for from $12.00 to $15.00. It is a triumph of the decorators' art. It is impossible for us to do it justice by description. Weight, packed 30 lbs.
Price.............$8.10

---

thought people would be shot across the country through tubes by 1975. Ray Stannard Baker, a respected magazine reporter, considered the infant automobile and saw it making the city a better place in which to live: "It is hardly possible to conceive of the appearance of a crowded wholesale street in the day of the automotive vehicle. In the first place, it will be almost as quiet as a country lane—all the crash of horses' hoofs and the rumble of steel tires will be gone. And since vehicles will be fewer and shorter than the present truck and span, streets will appear less crowded."

Though they found such predictions of things to come very interesting, Americans at the turn of the century felt that they were living in a very good present. The overriding mood of the times was one of unalloyed optimism; not only was all well with the world, but the world was getting better and better. The antics of society became more expensively lavish than ever as the wealthy sought to outdo each other: one gave a horseback dinner at which the guests ate while mounted on live horses in the ballroom; another had a waterfall installed in his dining room for a party; a Newport hostess invited guests to a party to meet a "Prince del Drago," who turned out to be a monkey in evening dress. This was the period when John Jacob Astor opined: "A man who has a million dollars is as well off as if he were rich." The public followed the didos of the rich with interest and possibly some envy, but with no resentment. Even the farmers, victims of low prices and foreclosed mortgages for years, were harvesting bumper crops and enjoying higher prices.

But not everything was bright. The Census Bureau reported in 1905 that the working class was very far from sharing in the general well-being; it estimated that the average worker earned $523.12 a year, though $800 was accepted by sociologists as the minimum on which a family could live decently. To earn their pittance, workers had to toil eighty, ninety, or one hundred hours a week, often in the most wretched conditions in unsafe mines or among unprotected machinery. To supplement family income children worked; the census of 1900 found that four out of every hundred workers on nonfarm jobs were children between ten and fifteen. Many were younger, for in most states it was completely legal to put a child of any tender age in a factory and work him as long as he could stay awake.

The Negro was another who failed to appreciate that he was living in the best of worlds. He had long since been deprived of his right to vote in the South by intimidation and deceit. In 1896 the Supreme Court made its landmark "separate but equal" decision, which gave its blessing to segregation by ruling that a law requiring separate facilities for Negroes did not constitute discrimination as long as the facilities were equal to those provided whites. The white South seized on the part of the doctrine sanctioning separateness and completely ignored the requirement for equality. In 1900 the Negro was less than a second-class citizen. When President Theodore Roosevelt had Booker T. Washington, the nation's most eminent Negro, to dine at the White House the cries of outrage, from North as well as South, would have led an outsider to believe the republic was tottering. "The most damnable outrage ever committed by a citizen of the United States," was a typical comment on the President's action by the Southern press.

The most portentous phenomenon of the first years of the century was the development of the horseless carriage into a practical automobile. In 1900, when the auto makers were just getting the feel of their new industry, twelve companies turned out 4,192 machines. In 1910, 187,000 automobiles—electrics and steamers as well as gasoline-burners—came from the shops of sixty-nine makers. Early motoring was more a sport than a means of transportation, for there were few roads worthy of the name outside the cities, and the first automobiles were so temperamental that the driver also had to be a capable mechanic. But as motorists competed in hill climbs, races, and city-to-city reliability runs, pitting their Toledos, Panhards, Duryeas, Locomobiles, Wintons, and Stanley Steamers against each other, weaknesses in design and construction were gradually detected and eliminated. As early as 1903 two men made a coast-to-coast trip in their Packard in fifty-two days, a feat that merits respect because there were no roads over long sections of the route in the West. And in 1908 there was an incredible race from New York to Paris by way of Alaska and Siberia, a route with hundreds of untracked miles. An early plan to cross Bering Strait by driving on the ice was discarded as impractical, and the cars were ferried over. A German and an American entry finished the race; the American, a Thomas Flyer, won, and for this feat alone deserves something better than the oblivion into which history has cast this once proud machine.

The automobile during those early years was largely a plaything of the wealthy. Motoring was too expensive except for the prosperous, and besides, the machines made a lot of noise and smell and frightened horses. The president of Princeton University, Woodrow Wilson, took occasion in 1907 to warn his students against the motorcar: "Nothing has spread socialistic feeling in this country more than the use of the automobile. . . . To the countryman they are a picture of arrogance of wealth, with all its independence and carelessness." However, Henry Ford produced his first Model T in 1908, and soon the automobile would be within reach of Everyman.

This was also the decade when man took to the sky in a heavier-than-air contraption. In 1903 Wilbur and Orville Wright lifted their fragile assemblage of wires and struts and fabric briefly over the dunes of North Carolina using the power of a gasoline engine. It was a momentous occasion that would have revolutionary results, but unlike the automobile, many years would pass before the plane would intimately affect the lives of the American public.

This was the golden era of the interurban electric lines, the trolleys that not only whisked people from city to city but also carried light freight and picked up farmers' milk at crossings for delivery to the creamery. The interurban cars were usually built a little heavier than city streetcars; many had baggage compartments, and some of the more thriving ones had dining cars. One or two of the longer lines even

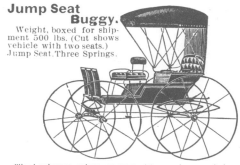

offered sleeping-car service. For a few brief years the interurbans were a threat to the railroads, for tracks to carry the light trolleys could be laid down for a fraction of what it cost to build roadbed for a steam train. The hoot of the interurbans' air whistles sounded from coast to coast, but they were most numerous north of the Ohio River, where the flat land made it possible to lay rails almost anywhere along country roads or across meadows.

The American love affair with baseball was in full swing during the first years of the century. Almost every small town with nine healthy young men had its team, and there were scores of very minor prairie and valley and river leagues whose names are now forgotten but whose rivalries were once very important to loyal and vociferous fans. It is not surprising that "Take Me Out to the Ball Game" was written during this era (1908) and became an all-time popular song hit. Though the National League had been a going concern since 1876, the American League did not take shape until 1901. The pennant winners of the two leagues met in the first World Series in 1903.

College football, on the other hand, had not yet captured the imagination of the masses, though it was gaining in popularity. As far as the East was concerned, football did not exist in the Midwest and South: newspaper accounts of games dealt at length with Princeton, Yale, and Harvard, and might give lesser mention to such schools as Cornell, Pennsylvania, and Columbia. The principal reason for this bias was that football meetings between Yale, Harvard, and Princeton were not merely games, they were major society events. On the day of such a contest, trains pulling special parlor cars freighted with names from the social register rolled toward Cambridge or New Haven or Princeton. Eastern dominance of—and myopia toward—football is indicated by the selections of Walter Camp for his All-American teams. In 1902, for instance, a very good year for Yale in the three-cornered rivalry, Yale placed seven men, Harvard two, and Princeton one on the mythical team. An Army player, by dint of exceptional ability and effort, was also included among the immortal eleven.

Among other sports, lawn tennis had been long established as a woman's game as well as a man's, but it was beginning to take on a bit more verve; even the ladies were starting to make vigorous swipes at the ball instead of gently lobbing it back and forth as they tripped about holding their skirts with one hand. Golf was relatively new at the turn of the century—at least as an American game—but it became popular after William Howard Taft, a golf enthusiast, became President in 1909. Despite his three-hundred-pound bulk and Theodore Roosevelt's advice against being photographed playing such an unmanly game (Roosevelt had definite ideas on what was manly and unmanly), Taft played often and openly, and the public eagerly adopted golf.

During the early years of the 1900's that American self-improvement phenomenon, the Chautauqua movement, reached its peak. The movement had had its beginning in 1874, when a group of Sunday-school teachers met at a camp on the shores of Lake Chautauqua in New York to discuss the Bible and how to teach it. They also discussed some matters of secular interest. The camp turned into a permanent summer colony over the years, and its offerings included summer courses in many subjects—arts, crafts, music, domestic science. As many as twenty-five thousand persons attended a session. Even so, the cultural facilities of this little Athens in western New York State were available to only a small portion of the American public until shortly after 1900, when a lecture bureau promoted traveling Chautauquas, tent shows that brought a week or so of self-betterment to the hinterlands. Families came by farm wagon and buggy for miles, often to spend several nights sleeping in tents so that they might spend their days in an almost pathetic grasping after culture, listening to lectures on everything from Christian behavior to home canning. The program was also liberally sprinkled with such diversions as jugglers, vocal numbers, dramatic "readings," and the like. The tent shows flourished for a dozen years or so, then gradually declined.

In spite of the absorption with self-improvement, these were not years when higher education was held in particularly lofty esteem by the workaday world. It was a pragmatic era, the self-made man was admired, and business was deemed the ideal career for a young man. Of a number of railroad executives interviewed for an article in a 1902 issue of *The Saturday Evening Post*, not one believed that a college education was necessary to a career in railroading; and there were some who thought it would be detrimental by causing a young man to lose four precious years in getting started in the field. Steel magnate Charles E. Schwab also believed that a college education was a disadvantage to a businessman. Russell Sage, multimillionaire money manipulator, was even more suspicious of learning: he thought that a mind filled with extraneous knowledge could not concentrate on the main business of making money. "With many of us," he wrote, "in fact most of us, I believe it would be better if we were turned into the active work of the world at fifteen or sixteen." In this atmosphere most youths who went to college did so to study law or medicine or other professions, or to prepare for cloistered careers behind college walls as zoologists or botanists or philosophers.

The number of women in college was increasing, though it was far below the enrollment of men. In other fields women were breaking old patterns of repression. They had won the vote in four Western states. They had made themselves indispensable in business, albeit in the subordinate position of stenographers and secretaries. They were driving automobiles about city streets, although the mayor of Cincinnati, in his wisdom, announced in 1908: "No woman is physically fit to run an auto." A Methodist bishop revealed that giving women the vote would deprive men of a proud privilege: "It is his glory to represent her. To rob him of that right would weaken both." In 1904 a woman was arrested in New York for smoking a cigarette in the back seat of an automobile. It was a hopeless gesture, for women were going to gain much more than the right to smoke during the next few years.

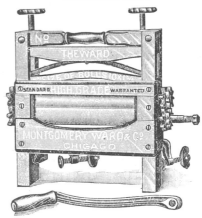

Our "Ward" Wringer.
WARRANTED 3 YEARS.

C 5700 The "Ward" wood frame Wringer is made exactly like the illustration, with hard wood frame, steel pressure spring and high-grade rubber rolls. It turns easily and does perfect work on either thick or thin material. Diameter of rubber rolls, 1¾ in.; length, 10 in. Warranted three years for family use. Entire wringer is handsomely finished, and price is as low as can be made, consistent with good material and workmanship. Approximate weight, 14 lbs. Each......................$2.00

Colored Lens Spectacles.
Without Focus.

23532— Coquille Spectacles for weak eyes, shell shaped, smoke or blue lenses, straight temples, steel frame, ordinary quality. Price....................................$0.20

Trimmed Hats.

18724 Corrine. Fine black silk lace hat, with jet edge, crown and band; trimmed with wide fancy silk ribbon, rhinestone buckle, large spray of fine velvet and muslin flowers and velvet forget-me-nots. Each......................$5.00

IN THE CITY

The Flatiron Building (at left, photographed while under construction in 1901) was far from the tallest building in New York when it went up, but it was considered a masterpiece of skyscraper engineering, and its peculiar shape won it a special place in the affections of the people of the city. Erected in what was then the glittering center of town on a sharply triangular plot where Broadway angles across Fifth Avenue, it was first named the Fuller Building, but its odd shape quickly caused New Yorkers to give it the name it has borne ever since. The busy scene above is South Water Street, then Chicago's market area, looking west from Dearborn, sometime between 1900 and 1910. A market is a busy and crowded place under the best of circumstances; this picture shows how the confusion is compounded when all transportation is by horse-drawn vehicles.

MILL AND FACTORY

Industrialization was attracting more and more Americans from the home and the farm into factories. By today's standards many of the results were sad; the little girl above worked long hours in a South Carolina cotton mill in 1909 before effective child labor laws were adopted. The women at top right are at work in a salmon cannery in Portland, Oregon; women too were working in factories. The men at bottom right are Russian steel workers at Homestead, Pennsylvania; many of the new immigrants from eastern Europe were supplying the unskilled labor for such industries as mining and steel.

OVERLEAF: The automobile, which was about to change American life styles and values as much as industrialization, was being tested. This lonely machine, photographed somewhere in the West, is on a Packard "reliability run" in 1903 from San Francisco to New York. It was only the second automobile to cross the United States; its time: sixty-three days.

AMERICAN AUTOMOBILE ASSOCIATION

DOWN ON THE FARM

The very beginning of the twentieth century was almost the last moment when farmers were still a majority of the American population. In 1900 more people lived in the country than in all the big cities, medium-sized towns, and small villages combined. Before the 1910 census the balance shifted. Farmers were in a minority for the first time since the republic was formed. The musical couple at right were photographed in 1904. They were settlers in Comanche County, Kansas, and it is plain that the good prairie soil, under the urging of their own hard work, has been good to them, for they live in a comfortably furnished house and have a piano. The scene above is another of Chansonetta Stanley Emmons' studies of rural Maine; her meager notation says only that Mrs. True is handing a dipper of water to Mr. True atop the hay. Chansonetta Emmons, incidentally, was the sister of the twin Stanley brothers who, among other things, invented the fabled Stanley Steamer automobile.

116

This scene of apparently confused activity is, in fact, a very well organized threshing crew at work during a wheat harvest. The place is probably Kansas; it could as well be Minnesota, the Dakotas, or any one of the wheat-growing prairie states. Later, between the two World Wars, the combine, which cuts and threshes grain in one operation, became general in the Midwest as it had earlier in the West, and scenes such as this are now only nostalgic memories.

OVERLEAF: *E. E. Smith was a cowboy as well as a photographer, and his pictures of cattle and of the cowpunchers who took care of them are among the best we have. In this one, which he made of a herd on the Matador Range in Texas, one can almost feel the dust. When this picture was made in 1909, the great days of cattle ranching were past, most of the open range had been fenced, and cattle-raising was more economically competitive than physically challenging.*

TO LIGHTEN WOMAN'S WORK

The mail-order catalogue was making things difficult for the back-country peddler and door-to-door salesman, but there was still a living to be made by a man who knew how to push his line by personal salesmanship. The gentleman above is hawking his stoves in Michigan about 1900, and is going where his market is, down the back roads away from towns and cities. His farm family audience seems interested in his spiel for the improved Home Monarch kitchen range and is impressed by his demonstration of its sturdiness as he whacks it with a hatchet. The girl on the opposite page—possibly a young bride—was photographed with her ultramodern washing machine in Leavenworth, Kansas, in 1900. It seems not to have been a picture made for advertising purposes; apparently the young lady was so proud that she wanted to be photographed with her new possession.

122

The barbershop was still exclusively a male retreat in the early 1900's. This is the establishment of Rudy Sohn in Junction City, Kansas, in 1903, correct in every detail from the neatly ranked shaving mugs of regular customers to the striped shirts, the parted hair, and the bay rum aroma in the shop.

OVERLEAF: *The first World Series was played in 1903. This is the seventh game in Boston, which had to be stopped twice when excited crowds surged onto the field. The Boston Americans won when Bill Dineen struck out Honus Wagner of the Pittsburgh Nationals.*

14. A COASTING PARTY ON THE CRIPPLE CREEK SHORT LINE.
PHOTO. BY McCLURE, DENVER.

A TIME FOR FUN

The fashionably dressed group at left is identified as a "coasting party on the Cripple Creek Short Line," a route that served one of Colorado's rich mining regions. As to their peculiar sport, we can only guess, but it appears that they are about to roll downhill from where they are under the urging of gravity. There is no question about what the trio in the boat above are doing; they are simply out to enjoy New York's beautiful Lake Minnewaska.

The magnificent backdrop against which these three young couples are posing is Leatherstocking Falls near Cooperstown, New York. The year is 1903. Like every picnic or outing group ever photographed before the 1920's, these people are dressed almost as though for church; the only hint of informality is that one daring young man has shed his coat.

CONCERNING WOMEN

There is something about a lovely woman that can make even the most ridiculous of hats seem completely right and proper when she is wearing it. The lady above, serenely self-assured under a confection of ostrich plumes that resembles a small haycock, sat for her portrait in Leavenworth, Kansas. The pensive study at left was made about 1900; the location is unknown but was probably somewhere on Long Island when most of that region was still farm and woodland.

133

WEDDINGS

We are told that in heaven there is no giving or taking in marriage, but it always has been a very popular institution on earth. Moreover, it is a much-photographed one, for people who otherwise seldom give much thought to having their picture taken tend to be sentimental about having a record of their wedding. The tableau above is familiar, although the bride does not often have such a commanding platform from which to throw her bouquet to the young single ladies below. The wedding was in 1908 near Cooperstown, New York. The earnest young couple at the right were married at Crookston, Minnesota, in 1900; here, after the wedding, they sit for their formal portrait.

The women above are decorating the house for a New Year's reception; the engraving appeared in a magazine of January, 1878. The young lady with muff (opposite) brightens an early Christmas card.

136

Some American Holidays

Americans celebrate many holidays throughout the year. Some are national, some regional. Some, such as Washington's Birthday, pay homage to great men; others, like Independence Day, commemorate notable events; still others, such as Memorial Day, honor defenders of the nation. The most venerable of American holidays is Thanksgiving, which stems from the day in 1621 when the Pilgrims put aside their work to express gratitude for blessings received. Though they were not the first settlers in America to proclaim a day of thanksgiving, their manner of celebrating with a feast of native foods is the one that survives and makes Thanksgiving a uniquely American holiday.

Citizens of different states do not always celebrate the same holidays. Lincoln's Birthday, for instance, is not observed in the Deep South, while only the Southern states commemorate the birthday of Robert E. Lee. Among holidays peculiar to a single state are Fast Day in New Hampshire, Seward's Day in Alaska, Andrew Jackson's Birthday in Tennessee, Mecklenburg Day in North Carolina, Pioneer Day in Utah, and a half a hundred more.

Days take on special meanings for strange and often unknown reasons. No one knows why the church festival of Candlemas became Ground-Hog Day in the United States about a century ago. On the other hand, holidays fade away. Once New Yorkers celebrated Evacuation Day, the anniversary of the British departure in 1783, as spiritedly as they did Independence Day. But New York, which ceaselessly discards the old for something newer and bigger, has long since forgotten Evacuation Day. There have been other losses. Fifty years ago children made and filled paper baskets with candy on May Day, and after dusk left them on the doorsteps of mystified friends. Possibly in some corner of America children still deliver May baskets in the spring night, but more likely this is a completely vanished rite of spring.

137

The character of Independence Day celebrations has changed greatly with the years; this colored print of F. A. Chapman's "Independence Day" pictures the Fourth in an era when pleasures were simpler and patriotic observances more enthusiastic. At the left are two Fourth of July cards from the late nineteenth century; at that time people still exchanged greetings on the Fourth.

OVERLEAF: *Doris Lee's 1935 painting of a farm kitchen during the Thanksgiving dinner rush treats a time-honored subject humorously.*

Eternal Love.

St Valentine 1847.

The two valentines at the upper left are among the early tokens of love produced by the young American greeting-card industry, which came into being after the Civil War. After the turn of the century the card makers learned to take advantage of such occasions as Easter, Halloween, St. Patrick's Day, and Thanksgiving. Directly left is a Currier and Ives lithograph of the 1870's called "Snap Apple Night," an old local dialectic name for Halloween. The colored engraving above of young people making Christmas wreaths is by Winslow Homer.

During World War I Childe Hassam made twenty-four paintings of flag-decked New York. This one, "Allied Day, May, 1917," shows Fifth Avenue. "Over There" (opposite) was a favorite war song.

The End of Innocence: 1910-19

Those who lived during the dozen or so years immediately preceding the First World War tend to remember it through a kind of golden haze as the best of all eras in American history. And for a good part of the American public it was a pleasant time. The world was at peace, and there was confidence that it would remain at peace because man had at last outgrown the savagery of war. There was a new social awareness in the land that was manifesting itself in such movements as those urging the outlawing of child labor and the regulation of health and safety conditions in factories. The national mood was one of unbounded confidence that the future could only get brighter. All was not idyllic, but there was a conviction that existing wrongs could and would be righted. Then in August, 1914, war broke out in Europe and shattered the illusion that an age of peace and felicity had arrived. The pleasant way of life was lost beyond recall, for by the time the war was over new times and new ways were in the ascendancy.

Those last prewar years saw the twilight of old-time small-town America. The nation, for all its industrialization and urbanization, was still predominantly rural and small-town in 1910; of its population of 92 million, considerably more than half lived on farms, in hamlets, villages, or small towns. It was a horse-and-buggy era; although there were some automobiles about, they belonged mainly to the prosperous, and the clop of horses' hoofs was still a familiar sound on tree-shaded streets. On Memorial Day, when the small parades wound down dirt roads to village cemeteries and old men reminisced about the War, they meant the Civil War. People who traveled did so by railroad; by scheduled train it was possible to reach hundreds of flag stops on branch lines that today have not seen a passenger train in many years. Sunday churchgoing was almost universal, and only in the cities had there been any noticeable erosion of old-time religious customs.

Patriotic Flag Outfits

Consisting of cotton flag with sewed stripes and printed stars, canvas heading and metal grommets. Jointed pole with truck ball and halyard and galvanized flag pole holder packed in cardboard box. Ship. wt., about 4 lbs.
60B6160—Size, 3x5 feet. Each....**$2.00**
60B6162—Size, 4x6 feet. Each.....**3.00**

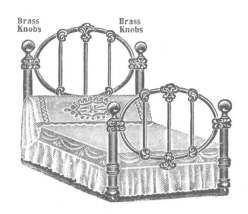

This is a very plain and neat design, and is a good solid bed for the price. Made entirely of iron and finished white enamel, or any plain color desired. Decorated in gilt.

$343

4W6104

$58⁵⁰ Genuine Raccoon

Length, 52 inches.
Sizes, 38 to 48 inch chest.
Mention Size Wanted.

The outside fur of this garment is a genuine Raccoon. Also has large Raccoon collar and cuffs. Pocket tops trimmed with Coon tails. Lined throughout body with close quilted, heavily padded sateen. Striped sleeve lining. Leather arm shields. Deep vent in back. Closes with two rows of loops and buttons. Knit wristlets. Average weight, 11 lbs.

The automobile was to be the principal agent of destruction of this easygoing way of life. In 1908 Henry Ford produced his first Model T. The cheapest model, a two-seat runabout, sold for $825, and though there were other makes at a comparable price, there were none as ruggedly built for less than about $1,500. After Ford introduced mass production the price fell sharply, to less than $500 in 1914 and down to $260 for the runabout by 1925. During these years Model T production soared, from ten thousand in 1909 to a quarter of a million in 1914 (almost half of all automobiles made that year) to more than a million in 1916 and two million in 1923.

The Model T put America on wheels. It was within the reach of most pocketbooks. It was sturdy enough to travel on poor roads, upkeep and repair were easy, and it could serve a farmer for light hauling as well as pleasure. With the proliferation of the automobile came a demand for all-weather roads, and as a web of improved auto routes gradually spread across the country an increasingly mobile population changed its patterns of living and shopping, vacationing, and even courting. The results were changes in social habits and accelerated shifts in populations, with some communities thriving and growing and others shriveling away. These, however, were effects of the automobile age that would not be fully revealed until the twenties.

Americans grumbled over the first income tax in 1913, but not very loudly, for its first impact was not too painful; had they been able to look ahead there probably would have been an outcry from ocean to ocean. The Supreme Court in the past had struck down taxes based on income; the Sixteenth Amendment, ratified in 1913, made such a tax constitutional, and Congress at once passed an income-tax bill. It levied a graduated tax of one per cent on incomes over $3,000 for single persons and $4,000 for married persons, with surtaxes beginning at one per cent on net incomes between $20,000 and $50,000 and going up to 6 per cent on incomes of more than half a million dollars. A married man earning $20,000 would have to pay a tax of about $160. Those easy days would not last long, and the income tax would prove a powerful instrument for social change through redistribution of wealth. During the First World War citizens learned how hard the tax could bite: rates rose sharply in all brackets, with the normal tax starting at 6 per cent and the surtax going in rapid steps up to 65 per cent.

In many ways the decade was the beginning of America's entry into the modern age in which we still live, the era marked by a breaking away from traditions and customs and a willingness to experiment with the new in everything from art forms to human relations. In 1905 when Shaw's *Mrs. Warren's Profession*, a moralistic study of prostitution, first played in New York, it had been quickly shut down by the censor and condemned by critics. It would be gross exaggeration to say that public attitudes had changed radically within the next half-dozen years, but there were stirrings of a fresh wind. When J. M. Synge's *Playboy of the Western World* was produced in this country in 1911 its earthy language did cause protests in Philadelphia and New York, but there were no attempts to close the play.

The American public had its first confrontation with avant-garde art in 1913 when the famous Armory Show opened in New York. The show brought to the United States hundreds of European works of art —abstract, cubist, nonobjective, various radical approaches strange to American eyes—by such painters as Picasso, Matisse, and Cézanne. It was a startling experience for many Americans. The press, with no background for intelligent criticism, resorted to ridicule; its special target was Marcel Duchamp's "Nude Descending a Staircase," for in Duchamp's attempt to depict motion on canvas it was difficult to find either nude or staircase. On the road the show attracted huge crowds —400,000 viewed it in Chicago—and though most came out of curiosity, the show had a deep influence on young Americans who would become the postwar generation of artists.

More within the understanding of the general public was a conventional French painting brought to this country the year of the Armory show. Called "September Morn," it showed a pretty young girl about to skinny-dip, and though the most chaste of pictures, it was banned in New Orleans and received the attention of sin-fighter Anthony Comstock, who tried to prevent a New York art dealer from displaying the picture. Though Queen Victoria had long been in her grave, Victorianism was not yet dead.

Another turn toward the new and innovative was the development of a new folk style of music that gained sudden popularity as ragtime. In 1911 Irving Berlin's "Alexander's Ragtime Band," its syncopated beat taken from Negro jazz, was an instant success and brought a demand for more tunes in the same tempo. At the same time a succession of new dances became popular: the grizzly bear, the turkey trot, the bunny hug, all of which found the couples snuggled up to each other as they moved about the floor. Traditionalists shuddered and tried to turn back the clock and restore decorum, but the bunny huggers danced on. In the summer of 1914 the rhythm changed and the South American tango took over. Couples tangoed not only on the dance floor but at home, on the beach, even in the streets. Then, like every fad, it spent itself.

A further sign of changing mores was a more relaxed attitude toward smoking and social drinking among women. The change was first noticeable in the cities, particularly those in the East. Although in many rural regions old women serenely puffed on corncob pipes, the heartlands looked on a woman who smoked cigarettes or drank as fallen beyond redemption. In metropolitan cafés, however, the sight of a young woman coolly joining her escort in a cocktail and cigarette was becoming common enough not to shock. Cigarette smoking had increased 500 per cent between 1900 and 1914 in spite of being considered "sissy" as well as unhealthy for men; without any medical knowledge of their actual effects the public was certain that cigarettes were bad for the lungs and called them coffin nails.

Into this world, pleasantly content with the present yet changing more than it realized, came word of the outbreak of war in Europe. The first reaction was one of shock and disbelief, so sure was the

12B351

Hemp, Ostrich Pompon, Aigrette Effect, Velvetta Ribbon—Price, $2.50

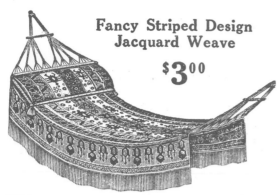

American public that there could be no more wars. The nation was torn between Allies and Germans by strong tides of sympathy, but the prevailing sentiment was that the war was none of America's business. Nevertheless, as time passed and the issues became clearer, national feeling swung overwhelmingly toward the Allies. In April, 1917, the United States entered the war.

The nation threw itself vigorously into winning the war. It sent the best of its young men abroad, and most of them went with enthusiasm, singing "Over There" and "There's a Long, Long Trail A-Winding." At home, industry and farmers were mobilized to produce more weapons and food. Citizens were exhorted to buy war bonds—and bought generously. There were meatless days, wheatless days, substitutes for familiar foods; women rolled bandages; children saved peach pits for gas-mask filters. A Committee of Public Safety was formed to whip up hate against the enemy and used speeches, posters, motion pictures, and every other available medium to tell of German brutality and depravity. The results were both effective and frightening. The teaching of German in schools and colleges was banned. German music, even that of such immortals as Wagner and Beethoven, was proscribed. Sauerkraut was renamed "liberty cabbage." Every person with a German (or unidentifiable) accent became suspect; every citizen of German ancestry, no matter how proven his loyalty, was fair game for amateur spy-snoopers or neighbors with a grudge.

The fighting ended in November of 1918 but the habit of hating remained, only now it was turned on a new target, the Bolsheviks, or Communists. Lawless acts were committed in the name of law and order; private citizens wrapped themselves in the flag and went on witch hunts. The Attorney General of the United States set the pace by embarking on an indiscriminate campaign against "reds," raiding without warrant homes, union headquarters, and other meeting places of alleged radicals. He was applauded at first, but by the spring of 1920 the better sense of the public began to reassert itself; when he alerted the National Guard to face revolutionary violence on May Day and nothing happened, there were titters. The red scare faded, but the hatemongering left a long legacy of anti-Semitism, Ku Klux Klan night riding, and other forms of bigotry.

Racial tension, too, had grown easily and naturally in the climate of suspicion and alienation engendered during the war. Many black people had migrated from the South to work in Northern war industries, and resentment by whites led to friction and violence. In 1917 forty-seven people, most of them blacks, were killed in race riots in East St. Louis, Illinois. In Washington troops had to be called out to help police end days of rioting between blacks and whites during July, 1919. In Chicago in the summer of 1919 an incident at a bathing beach involving black and white boys exploded into almost a week of racial war that left twenty-three Negroes and fifteen whites dead, more than five hundred people injured, and a thousand homeless.

Two amendments were added to the Constitution soon after the end of the war. One, the Eighteenth, was based on the assumption that an

148

entire nation's drinking habits were a subject for legislation. During the war the production of beer and liquor had been curtailed to save grain; the powerful antisaloon forces were able to have the temporary prohibition proposed as a permanent one in the form of a constitutional amendment, which was ratified in January, 1919, and went into effect a year later. It would change the drinking habits of millions of Americans, but not quite in the way they had anticipated.

The other amendment, the Nineteenth, ratified in August, 1920, gave women the right to vote. It ended a long battle that for much of the time had been fought by a small band of lonely pioneers. Progress had been glacially slow until the first years of the nineteenth century, when a group of determined women adopted disruptive tactics: throwing stones at political meetings, entering exclusive restaurants without an escort and demanding to be seated (then unheard of), anything to get arrested, attract attention, and become martyrs.

In 1910 suffragette organizations demonstrated their strength for the first time by parading down New York's Fifth Avenue, but they were only a few hundred strong, and the male jeers and ribald remarks were loud. The next year there were three thousand marchers, and in 1912 fifteen thousand, including a contingent of more than six hundred men for woman suffrage. The parades spread to other cities. Picketing near the Capitol and White House eventually brought arrests, charges of police brutality, and a wave of public sympathy. It was what the ladies wanted; after that their eventual victory was assured and was merely a matter of time.

The woman suffrage leaders had envisaged a kind of three-party system: Republicans, Democrats, and Women. They saw themselves as holders of the balance of power, and from that position leading the nation into a new and bright world by cleaning up politics, ending prostitution, halting waste in government—doing all the things that had never been done in a world governed by men. That dream quickly proved an illusion. The women got their vote just in time for the election of 1920, and they cast their first ballot overwhelmingly for handsome, genial, slack-willed Warren G. Harding, whose administration was not notable for its contributions to ethical government.

A TIME NOW GONE

Life in the small towns of America still moved at a quiet and leisurely pace during the last years before World War I, but it was a tranquillity that would end all too soon, never to return. Above, a young man named Robert Hillyer and his bride pose for their picture just before the guests arrive for the wedding reception. The others are evidently the parents of bride and bridegroom. It was a June wedding in 1915 at Cooperstown, New York. The charming photograph at left shows a typical interior sometime during the second decade of the twentieth century.

OVERLEAF: Also out of a vanished past is this moment in a 1913 Memorial Day ceremony, once typical of a thousand small towns in prewar America.

THE AGE OF GASOLINE

During the decade of 1910–19 the automobile began to dominate American life, and Henry Ford was largely responsible. By 1915 he had produced a million of his Model T's, and thanks to his assembly line methods, his output was constantly increasing. He first used the technique in 1913; above, automobile bodies, assembled on one line, are being placed on chassis put together on another assembly line. On the opposite page are two faces of the automobile revolution. The motorcar clogged city streets by its sheer numbers (the thoroughfare with traffic inching along is New York's Forty-Second Street; Bryant Park and the Public Library are on the right). On the other hand the automobile gave its owner mobility for business or pleasure. The happy family is out for a spin in what appears to be a Hupmobile, about 1911.

Building a sturdy and inexpensive automobile was only a part of the great enterprise of putting America on motorized wheels. The automobile needed all-weather roads to make it practical; the network of country roads that had served the horse and wagon well enough became impassable for motorcars when the rains came. Even in good weather some roads could be traversed only with dif-

ficulty, as this picture proves. The cars are crossing the Smoky Hill River in Kansas in 1919; at that time many streams were still crossed by fording. Though the picture seems at first glance to indicate that this was an all-male maneuver, closer inspection reveals what appears to be a lone woman, skirts tucked up, about midstream, lending what weight she can to the towline.

BY THE SEA

The history of women's bathing suits has been one of less and less. In the Victorian years a woman hardy enough to enter the water did so completely swaddled in many yards of cloth; pantalettes covered her lower legs, and she was expected to wear a corset. The mermaids here, shown playing in the surf at Easton's Beach in Newport, Rhode Island, about 1913, are hardly dressed for speed swimming, but their costumes have been streamlined considerably since that early time. The pantalettes, among other things, have been trimmed away, and it is a good guess that they are not wearing corsets. In another ten years there would be scandals on the beaches about one-piece knitted suits—and there is no need to detail what has happened to swimsuits more recently.

THE YOUNG EAGLES

From this distance in time, the aviators of the first couple of decades of this century seem almost quaint and old-fashioned, and their planes little more than antique toys. This is far from the truth: it took skill and daring to fly the early machines, and aviators risked their lives every time they took their antique toys off the ground. The pilot above is Max Lille, one of the pioneers; his happy passenger, whose garb seems more appropriate to dusting the house than aviating, is not identified. The picture at right is of the first international air meet to be held in the United States. The time was October, 1910, the place Belmont, Long Island, and the planes are, top to bottom, a Wright, a Farman, a Blériot, an Antoinette, and another Farman.

160

REQUIEM
FOR THE VILLAGE

These men, passing the summer hours in the shade of a scarred locust tree, were photographed in a small Indiana village in 1915. Once such scenes were common in villages and hamlets across America, but after the First World War the villages themselves began to languish and fade, and the process continues today. The automobile was the principal agent of the change, for it was seldom that the farmer or anyone else went to the crossroads store when his motorcar would take him to a better store in a big town in little more than a matter of minutes.

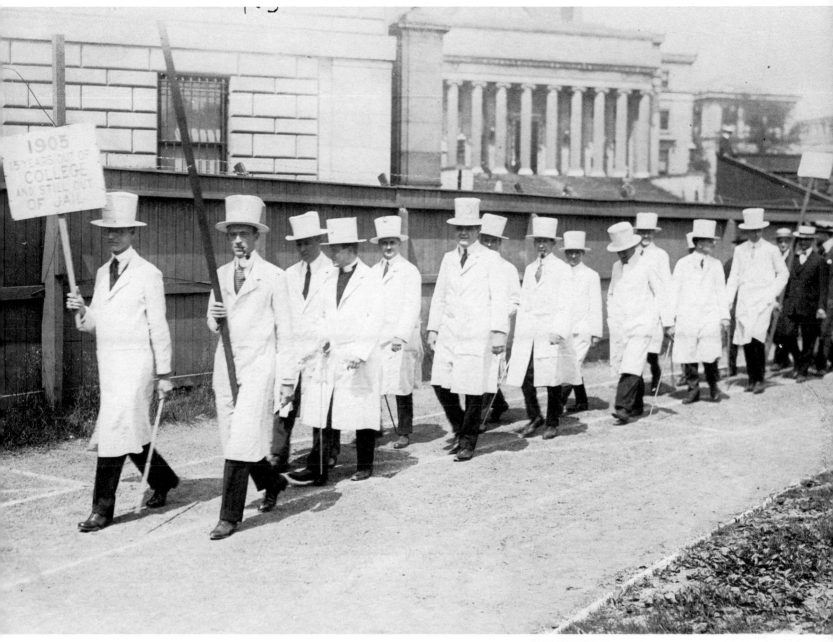

THE ASPECTS OF EDUCATION

Early American education was traditionally conservative, but by the twentieth century it was experimenting with things like manual training and music appreciation, which had nothing to do with the three R's. The girls at top left, for instance, are making water color pictures of flowers, something that in an earlier day would have been frowned on as frivolous. This is apparently a private school in what had once been someone's home; the place is probably New York. At bottom left the children of working mothers are being taught useful skills in a day nursery in 1915. And what has the parade above to do with education? It is the Columbia Class of 1905, marching proudly at a commencement reunion.

OVERLEAF: A horse-drawn school bus in Hinds County, Mississippi, stops along the road during an afternoon in 1915 to drop off passengers and have its picture taken.

FOREST

VOTES FOR WOMEN

The college women marching through downtown Philadelphia (above) in 1915 were only one of the contingents in a long parade demanding votes for women. There were similar demonstrations in other cities during this decade, until initial public ridicule gradually shifted to sympathy and support for female suffrage and finally gave women the vote in 1920. The lady at the left is sounding the call for assembly at a demonstration in Washington; the one on the right is modeling the recommended marching costume for the votes-for-women parade in Chicago on June 6, 1916.

168

I WANT YOU

for THE NAVY

AMERICA AT WAR

In 1917 the United States plunged into a major war. Starting almost from scratch, it recruited and put under arms nearly five million men during the next year and a half, and sent more than half of them overseas. Everything was done enthusiastically, from saving food to buying war bonds. Below is one of countless appeals for Red Cross volunteers; the organization had women busy doing everything from knitting socks to driving ambulances in France. At left is a Navy recruiting poster by Howard Chandler Christy, a prolific producer of such wartime art. And at right is an Irving Berlin song sheet of the time, a ditty voicing the doughboy's unhappiness with reveille.

COLLECTION OF LESTER LEVY

NEW JERSEY HISTORICAL SOCIETY

The sea of humanity at left is the crowd at a Liberty bond rally at Wall and Broad streets in New York. The young women above with their Model T Ford ambulance are a volunteer Red Cross unit in France; such crews did yeoman service in all but front-line areas. Even baseball players (below) got into the spirit if not into combat; these are the Chicago White Sox in close-order drill during spring training in 1918—under the direction of a real Army sergeant.

OVERLEAF: Troops back from France in 1919 parade up New York's Fifth Avenue and pass a reviewing stand in front of the appropriately decorated Metropolitan Museum of Art.

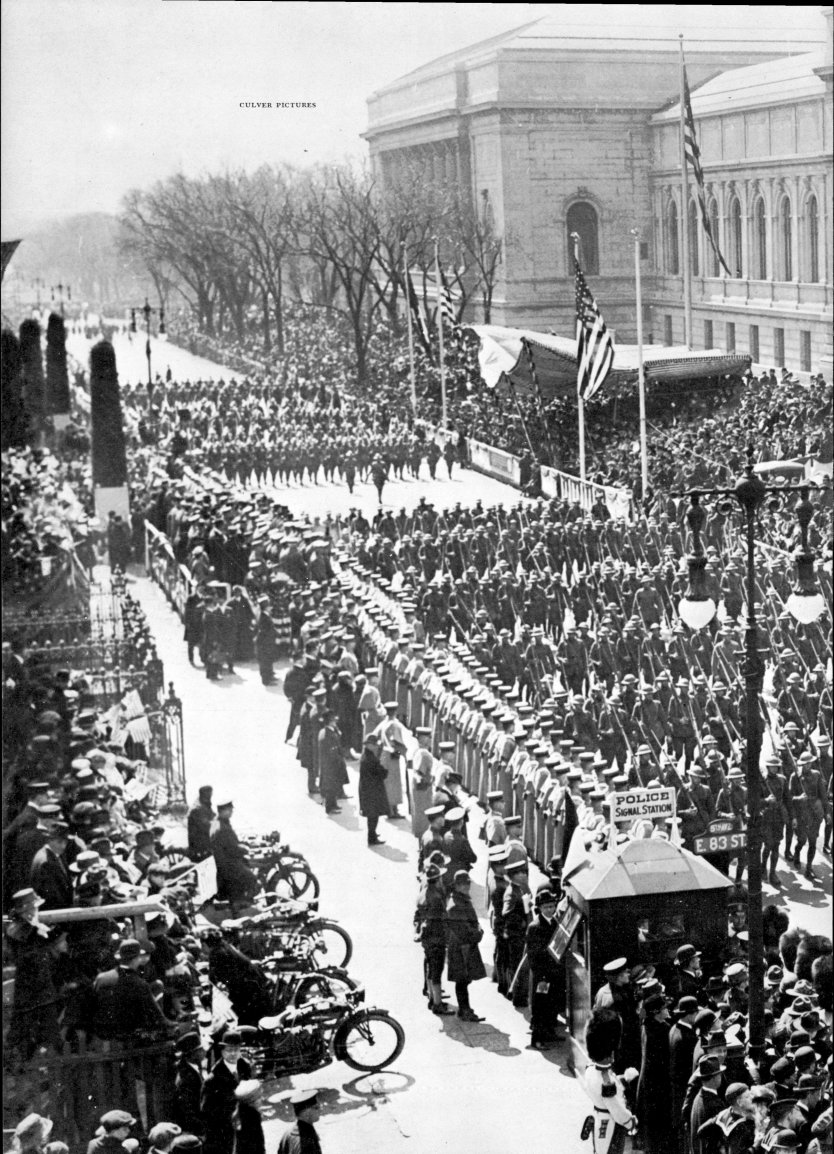

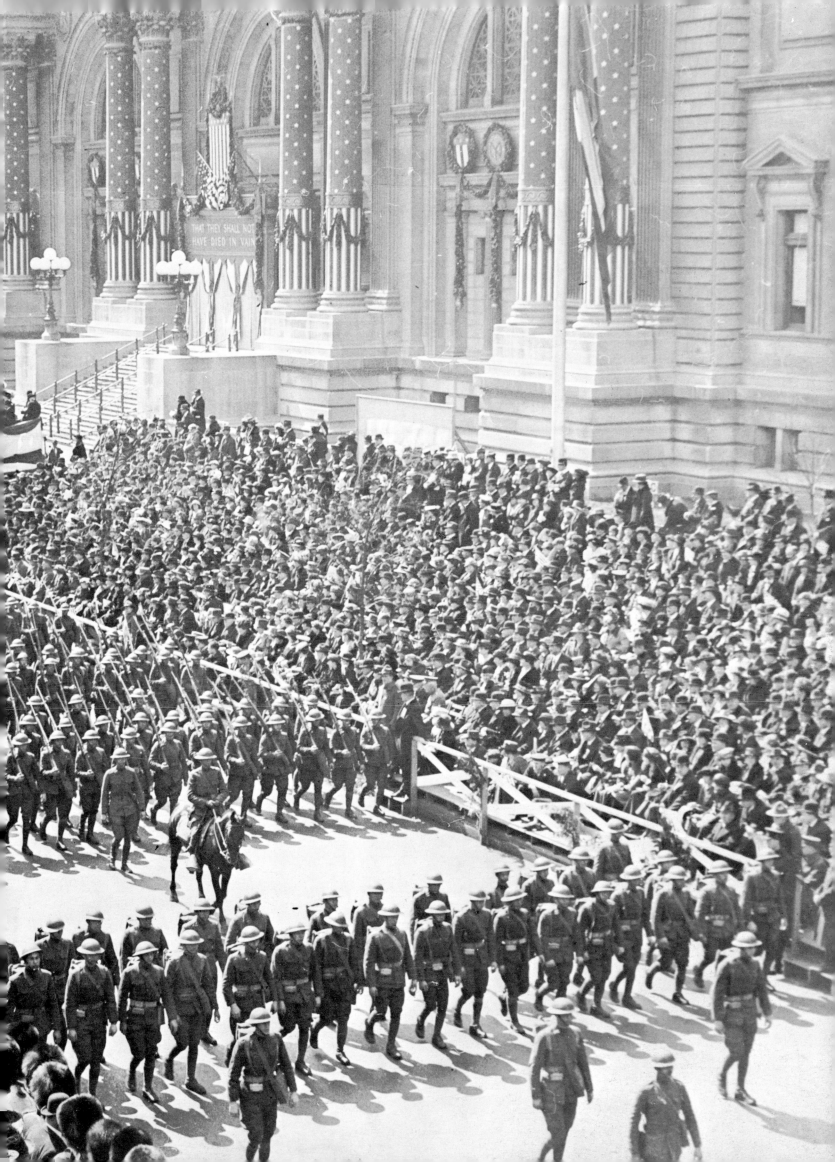

PIERRE BRISSAUD, *Fortune*, 1933

The speakeasy with a peephole in the door symbolized the prohibition era, and John Held, Jr., portrayed the flaming youth of the Jazz Age with his flappers (opposite, top) and coonskin-clad youths.

THE JAZZ AGE: 1920-29

Harper's Magazine, JULY, 1950

The 1920's have been dubbed the Jazz Age, but the decade was more than a time of flappers, saxophones, and coonskin coats. The twenties were a time of bewildering changes in American life; established patterns were breaking down on every hand, and flaming youth with its ukuleles and hip flasks was only one of many indications that things were no longer the way they once had been.

The American people had waged the First World War wholeheartedly. They had accepted meatless, wheatless, and sugarless days without complaint and had eaten strange substitute foods gamely, if not with relish, in the firm belief that they were thereby helping to defeat the Hun. They bought war bonds, they learned to hate the Kaiser passionately, and they agreed to Prohibition, but when the war was over they soon tired of sacrifices. They turned their backs on Europe, lost interest in the League of Nations, and elected Warren Harding, a genial man who called for no further sacrifices or strivings for a better world but comfortably promised a "return to normalcy."

But if returning to normalcy meant going back to things as they had been before the war, the people soon found that there was no turning back. Too many things had changed. An early casualty of the revolt against wartime austerity was Prohibition. There was no real attempt to repeal the dry laws—people simply ignored them. The sources of illegal liquor multiplied: it came across the border from Canada; it was landed at night in quiet coves along the coast by rum-running motorboats; it was produced in illicit distilleries and breweries; it came from the closets and basements of millions of American citizens who made strange-tasting home-brewed beers, bathtub gins, and home-fermented wines. The speakeasy was born, and the bootlegger became an important and necessary citizen of the community.

Prohibition agents were unable to cope with violations of the Eighteenth Amendment. They were undermanned: in 1920 there were only

Queen of This Page
"New Idea" Beauty

$3.98

512 B 61—Will fit heads 21¼ to 22½ inches. Ship. wt., 2 lbs. 4 oz. COLORS: Black; monkey skin (rose tan); gobelin (Copen) blue. State color wanted.

For the woman who demands the best—in quality, workmanship—and style. This delightful "suit-case" model is tailored with exaction from the fashionable Bengaline Cloth, dressed with gleaming Petaline Braid.

YOUTHFUL BLACK PATENT

24 D 20—Black patent.
SIZES: 2½ to 8. WIDTH: E. State size......**$1.89**
Postage 9¢
Increase order to $2 by including a pair of hose—
then we pay postage.
You'll be delighted with this Patent One-Strap with its
Chic beige underlays in the vamp cutouts. 1⅝-inch rubber-
topped heel. Fine leather sole. Leather insole. Worth $2.50.

$189

Three-Piece Outfit
Sweater, Knickers, Hose
$598
Ages 8 to 17

1,520 agents to guard all three coasts and the Canadian and Mexican borders, and in addition to seek out stills, speakeasies, breweries, and other violations; by 1930, when the tremendous scope of the job had long been apparent, the number had been increased only to 2,836. And they were underpaid: annual salaries that ranged between $1,200 and $2,000 in 1920 had risen only to $2,300 to $2,800 ten years later. Many agents succumbed to temptation and could be persuaded to look the other way when bootleg booze was being moved; the surprising thing is that so many agents continued to try to enforce a law that no one else seemed to care about.

The widespread flouting of the prohibition laws brought about a general lowering of respect for all law. People who had hardly touched liquor before took it up because it was the thing to do. Underworld elements quickly saw the huge profits to be made in bootlegging, and before long rival gangs were fighting for the privilege of peddling their beer and liquor to speakeasies. Murderous rivalries developed in all large cities, but the Chicago area led the way. More than five hundred gangland murders took place there during the twenties. Mobsters gained notoriety as the press played up syndicate crime. Al Capone, the most powerful of the Chicago hoodlums, gave orders to more than one politician, and by the end of the twenties he was worth millions of dollars. He was then thirty-two years old.

A phenomenon of the twenties was the public's eager acceptance of anything new, whether fad, sensation, or hero. Mahjong, a Chinese relative of rummy played with tiles, had become a national obsession by 1922. In 1923 Émile Coué arrived from France, and the country paused to listen and believe as he preached that the way to success and happiness would be opened simply by repeating the formula "Day by day in every way I'm getting better and better." In 1924 a young publisher brought out the first book of crossword puzzles, and within weeks the public was single-mindedly filling in blank spaces in puzzles. Sales of dictionaries soared; 60 per cent of the train travelers between Boston and New York were observed to be passing the time puzzling. Contract bridge, the Charleston, coonskin coats, and marathon dancing were among the other fancies of the time.

The public was sensation-hungry and was ably abetted by a press that had become skilled in the art of making the unimportant seem earth-shaking. Murder trials were made to seem events of the century. Notable were the Chicago trial of thrill killers Leopold and Loeb, the Hall-Mills trial in New Jersey, and the trial of Ruth Snyder and her paramour, Judd Gray. The last was an open-and-shut case, but it involved a sordid sex angle, and the newspapers gave it the biggest play yet; among the horde of reporters employed as special writers were cinema producer David Wark Griffith, actress Peggy Hopkins Joyce, author Will Durant, and evangelist Billy Sunday.

When John Scopes went on trial in the mountain town of Dayton for having taught, contrary to Tennessee law, the theory of evolution in his high school class, the surrounding ballyhoo made a Roman holiday of the event. And when an unknown young Kentuckian, Floyd

Collins, was trapped in a cave he was exploring, the entire country paused during the eighteen days of futile rescue efforts, and state troops and barbed wire were needed to hold back the crowds that gathered at the site.

Sports shared in the atmosphere of hysteria and sensationalism. Babe Ruth became the darling of the bleachers. Golfer Bobby Jones and tennis singles champions Big Bill Tilden and Helen Wills were national heroes. Gertrude Ederle became the first of her sex to swim the English channel and was rewarded with publicity beyond measure and a ticker-tape parade up Broadway. When Jack Dempsey took the heavyweight championship away from Jess Willard in 1919 the era of ballyhoo had not yet arrived, and not quite 20,000 fans saw the event; at the second Tunney–Dempsey match in 1927, 145,000 were present and paid $2,600,000 for the privilege. It is said that two thirds of those in the most distant seats did not know when the fight had ended. Red Grange of Illinois attained heights of football glory so towering that he was presented to President Calvin Coolidge, and one Notre Dame backfield was spoken of by such sportswriters as Grantland Rice as though its members were Homeric demigods rather than four very well coordinated but otherwise quite normal young men: "Outlined against a blue-gray October sky, the Four Horsemen rode again. In dramatic lore they are known as Famine, Pestilence, Destruction, and Death. These are only aliases. Their real names are Stuhldreher, Miller, Crowley, and Layden. . . ."

In 1927 a superhero arrived. He was Charles Lindbergh, and his feat was to fly nonstop from Long Island to Paris to win a cash prize. He was not the first man to fly the Atlantic—six dozen men had previously done that in planes and dirigibles—but he was the first to fly it alone, and by the time he landed in Paris he was already an immortal. Fortunately, he was an attractive, modest young man; he refused to boast in the slightest about his exploit, and he did not capitalize on it by accepting any of the flood of offers to make personal appearances, give testimonials, and the like, which would have made him a millionaire overnight. In return, America gave him an unlimited devotion such as it has granted to few, if any, other men. He received uncountable honors, had schools, streets, and babies named after him, and had an unbelievable amount of newspaper space devoted to him and to his flight, which one New York paper called "the greatest feat of a solitary man in the records of the human race." It was far from that, but Lindbergh was a much-needed relief from scandal, crime, and dollar-chasing heroes.

The twenties were good days for bankers and businessmen. Calvin Coolidge said, "The business of America is business," took long naps in the White House in the afternoon, and refused to rock the boat. For things were booming, and new products were quickening consumers' pulses. When the first broadcasting station went on the air in Pittsburgh to give the results of the 1920 Harding-Cox election, it was heard on crystal sets by a few amateurs, but before long radio had become one of the most absorbing fads of the twenties. Amateurs built their

Parisian Girdled Silhouette

New Idea in All-Silk Crepe Romaine
With All-Silk "De Luxe" Flat Crepe

14 B 75 Exquisite in every soft, clinging detail, this beautiful Frock brings you the latest message of French fashion artistry. A tribute to the NEW IDEA, told in heavy All-Silk Crepe Romaine, enhanced with a heavier touch of rich All-Silk "De Luxe" Flat Crepe.

own sets; people sat up half the night to log in as many stations from as far away as possible. It was a plaything with a dollar sign: by 1929 sales of radio sets and parts were edging up toward the billion-dollar mark; the 1922 sales had been only sixty million dollars.

Nothing, though, so affected the economy as the automobile. During 1920 somewhat more than eight million autos were registered; in 1929 the number was more than twenty-three million. This increase represented not only cars but gasoline, road construction, traffic control signals, and a host of other products that came into being because of the motor vehicle.

Automobiles and radio were only two leaders in a fast-moving economy. Total national production increased 34 per cent between 1922 and 1929, and the problem became one of getting the consumer to buy the wonders available to him. The salesman rather than the producer became the kingpin in business; the hard sell was admired, studied, and developed. Advertising took on a new sophistication, and the admen turned to psychology to appeal to the consumer's frustrations, social ambitions, and fears.

This materialistic approach to happiness was not universally popular; the so-called intellectuals rebelled against what they considered a crass and money-centered society. Novelist Sinclair Lewis was one of their early spokesmen; in his *Main Street* he depicted the small Midwestern town as a cultural desert, and in *Babbitt* he portrayed the American businessman as an insensitive, dull-witted booster type. Like all satires, it was one-sided—the small town and the businessman could have put up good counterarguments. Nevertheless, Lewis expressed what some people were feeling about contemporary society.

There was a revolt among youth, too, and a more spectacular one. The rebellion of the young people of the twenties, however, was not against the Establishment, as that of the late 1960's would be. They wanted their share of the good things that they saw around them, the shiny new cars, the best bootleg Scotch, a home in the new country-club district. But they were tired of old standards and thumbed their noses at them.

It was the women who went farthest in their rebellion, probably because they had farther to go. The flapper was soon raising glasses with her escort in speakeasies, sharing his hip flask at football games, lighting her cigarette from the same match. She began openly using rouge and lipstick, which her mother had considered something reserved for fallen women; she found the ancient corset confining so she threw it away; and her clothes became skimpier until her skirts reached the knee. She went to the barber, and her hair was cropped to a shingle bob. Along with all this, the younger generation discovered Sex. It was hardly unique to their generation, but they had the automobile in which to experiment, and they had Sigmund Freud, whose theories they learned just well enough to use glibly words like "libido" and "repression." What they did with their new sexual freedom only women now grandmothers can tell us, but it is on record that they talked about it endlessly.

180

The holiday spirit of the twenties did not reach everyone. There were many people who did not drink bootleg booze, did not dance the Charleston, did not share in the business boom. The great heartland of the country still supported Prohibition, read its Bible regularly, and hoped that God would smite the wicked big cities. Few farmers were making whoopee, for farm prices were in a slump during most of the twenties. And the short skirts and discarded corsets and abandoned petticoats spelled disaster to the textile industry of New England and the South.

A close look at the prosperity of the time shows how shallow it was. The Brookings Institution, a body of careful economists, found that in 1929, when the fired-up economy was at its peak, only slightly more than one family in fifty had an annual income of more than $10,000. At the same time, the Brookings economists fixed $2,000 as the minimum amount with which a family could provide its basic needs. Yet 60 per cent of American families were receiving less than that, and 42 per cent were getting less than $1,500.

Nevertheless, the prosperity wagon rolled on. The Big Bull Market on Wall Street got under way in 1926, and stock prices rose and rose. There were some warning voices, but many respected bankers and brokers were so exhilarated that they persuaded themselves that the market could rise indefinitely. The danger signals, however, were plentiful. The Florida land boom, ending in the bust of 1926, had been only the most spectacular of a number of land booms across the country that had led to wholesale mortgage foreclosures. The move to suburbia had caused a surge of home building, and the developers had done their work too well, for as the twenties drew near an end many new dwellings stood empty. Buying on the installment plan, many people had committed themselves far deeper than their incomes justified. And inventories of consumer goods were piling up all along the line, from factory warehouses to store shelves.

The shaky structure finally collapsed. Early in September, 1929, the Big Bull Market began slipping. It recovered, dropped again, steadied, and fell some more, while Wall Street talked about such things as technical adjustments. Then on October 24 the great crash came in a wild panic of selling. In that one day fourteen billion dollars in paper values were gone; by the time the market settled down three weeks later thirty billions had been wiped out. The twenties still had almost two months to run, but the Age of Jazz, the years of whoopee, was already dead and gone.

"HERE SHE COMES . . ."

The photo is undated, but these young ladies are probably displaying their charms in 1921, the year America discovered the bathing beauty contest. In July of 1921 there was a Costume and Beauty Show in Washington in which the girls were required to wear hats, tunic suits, and stockings (one girl rolled hers). In September of the same year the first beauty pageant was held in Atlantic City, and the girls were permitted to wear tight one-piece suits and to bare their legs. They have never gone back to wearing anything faintly like the outfits at the left.

THE OPEN ROAD

The elderly couple above contemplate the new Model T Ford that may, in 1921, have been their first venture into the breathtaking new age of the automobile. At right, above, is Nantasket Beach in Massachusetts on a Fourth of July in the early 1920's. Time has not solved the parking problem. And at bottom right is a stretch of the Lincoln Highway in Nebraska in 1929. This first coast-to-coast highway was opened from end to end in 1927, but, as the picture indicates, there were still sections that could hardly be called all-weather roads.

OVERLEAF: Though the auto gave new freedom to the adventurous, the open road was still only for the hardy. In some ways it offered more rewards then than now.

FLAMING YOUTH

Some of the actions of the flaming youth of the 1920's were a little silly, but the end results were far-reaching, for they created a revolution in manners and morals that swept away Victorianism. The party at the left is enjoying a radio at Grand Lake in the Colorado Rockies; dancing as close as this couple is doing was decried by the older generation as leading straight to moral collapse. The ukulele held by the girl above was essential equipment for the complete flapper. The time is early 1920's; they have not yet bobbed their long hair.

OVERLEAF: Jazz was the urgent voice of the liberated young generation; this band poses somewhat self-consciously on a New Jersey beach in 1922.

THE AD GAME

Prosperous America was producing a wealth of goods during the twenties, and the advertising business had much of the burden of making the public keep buying them. To do so it not only acquired new subtlety in its layouts, but it learned the art of motivation—it sold such things as youth, beauty, and glamour rather than the product. The ad at left and the one below say little about shirts or autos, but they do say much about elegance. The Listerine advertisement at the right was one of a long series based on the happy discovery that it is profitable to play on people's insecurities and self-doubts.

PIERCE-ARROW

Why had he changed so in his attentions?

THE thing was simply beyond her. She couldn't puzzle it out. And every moment it preyed on her mind and was almost breaking her heart.

He had been the most attentive lover and husband imaginable. But of late some strange something seemed to have come between them. Now he was so changed.

Was it some other woman? No, she told herself,—it *couldn't* be! Yet *why* wasn't he the way he used to be toward her?

* * *

That's the insidious thing about halitosis (unpleasant breath). You, yourself, rarely know when you have it. And even your closest friends won't tell you.

Sometimes, of course, halitosis comes from some deep-seated organic disorder that requires professional advice. But usually—and fortunately—halitosis is only a local condition that yields to the regular use of Listerine as a mouth wash and gargle. It is an interesting thing that this well-known antiseptic that has been in use for years for surgical dressings, possesses these unusual properties as a breath deodorant.

Test the remarkable deodorizing effects of Listerine this way. Rub a little onion on your fingers. Then apply Listerine and note how quickly the onion odor disappears.

This safe and long-trusted antiseptic has dozens of different uses: note the little circular that comes with every bottle. Your druggist sells Listerine in the original brown package only—three sizes: three ounce, seven ounce and fourteen ounce. Buy the large size for economy.—*Lambert Pharmacal Company, Saint Louis, U. S. A.*

FADS AND FOIBLES

The couple above are contestants in a marathon dance, one of the many crazes the public eagerly took up during the 1920's. The flappers at top right are entrants in a New York nightclub's Charleston contest in the heyday of that dance in 1926. And the society ladies at bottom right are at the Waldorf Astoria receiving their daily mahjong lesson by "radiomat" when that game was the current rage.

Prohibition was the most openly flouted law of the 1920's, if not of all American history, and gave the decade much of its reputation for lawlessness. At left, a rare photograph of a speakeasy interior proves that such places were not always glamorous. Above, protesters against the dry laws quote scripture in a 1921 anti-prohibition parade in New York. Below, federal agents destroy illicit beer.

The golden age of silent motion pictures was quite brief, from the time of the First World War until the mid-twenties. Above, a scene from The Unguarded Hour *with Milton Sills and Doris Kenyon is being filmed on location at a Greenwich, Connecticut, mansion. Note the violinist to provide mood music. The man below is Rudolph Valentino, heartthrob of millions of women, with Vilma Banky in* Son of the Sheik, *a picture released after the star's death in 1926. At left are the crowds waiting to see Al Jolson's* The Jazz Singer, *the first talking picture, which marked the beginning of the end of the silents in 1927.*

This is the first "million-dollar gate" of the sports-mad twenties—at Boyles Thirty Acres in New

Jersey when Jack Dempsey knocked out aging Frenchman Georges Carpentier in the fourth in 1921.

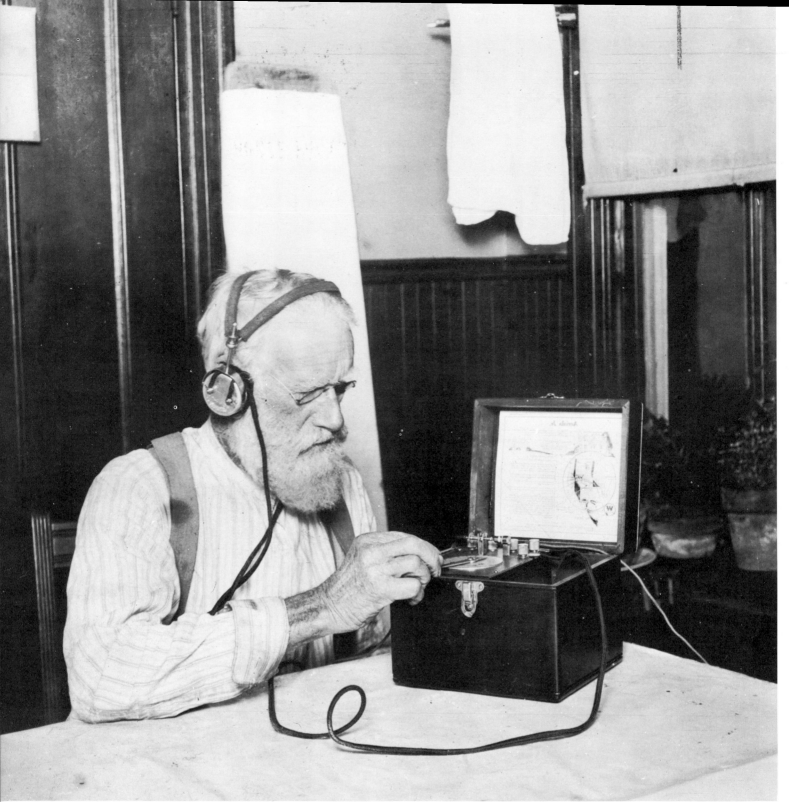

NEW ON THE HORIZON

Radio was still primitive and reception chancy in 1922 when the gentleman above tuned in his crystal set, for the first broadcast, the Harding-Cox election returns, had been made by station KDKA in Pittsburgh only two years earlier. Aviation, too, was still in its infancy, and barnstormers used their planes for such wing-walking stunts as the simulated tennis game at top right. Before long, airplanes began taking on much bigger responsibilities; the people at bottom right were photographed in a new ten-passenger Ford trimotor plane in 1927.

STATE HISTORICAL SOCIETY OF WISCONSIN

THE VIEW FROM HARLEM

Although blacks had been moving into the area for years before 1920, it was during the twenties that Harlem established its position as the Negro capital of America, the center of urban black culture, a neighborhood like many in New York except that it was larger and the faces darker. Above is a children's fashion show, the exact year uncertain. At right are three Harlem flappers of 1927.

STATUS QUO IN MIDDLE AMERICA

The moral and social upheavals of the twenties were phenomena chiefly of the East and of urban areas; middle America, with its basic conservatism, clung to old and tried values of family, fidelity, and religion. The family reunion above, representing probably four generations, typifies the solidarity that resisted radical change. The locale of the picture is unknown except that it is Midwestern; the time is the early 1920's. Midwestern farm families such as the one on the right explain why the Jazz Age seldom penetrated down country roads; such people did not carry hip flasks and make whoopee.

A century ago the art of James McNeill Whistler—in self-portrait here—was considered unorthodox; today modernists create such works as Josef Albers' "In Late Day (Homage to the Square)," at right.

A Century of American Art

American painting during the last hundred years has been as varied and inventive as the nation itself. In the last third of the nineteenth century, for instance, Americans admired the objective realism of Thomas Eakins, the poetic approach of James M. Whistler, Maurice Prendergast's impressionism, and the classical style of John La Farge. Elihu Vedder and Albert Ryder turned to the world of memory and dreams for themes, and John Singer Sargent produced innumerable elegant portraits.

Yet not one of these painters had his roots entirely in America; as they studied European painters and paintings they also developed a tendency to portray even American subjects in a European manner. Then in 1908 eight artists gave a historic exhibition in New York in which not only subjects but styles indicated American roots. Called the Ashcan School because they often turned to homely urban subjects previously scorned by artists, they opened the way for the development of native American painting.

By the 1930's American painting vigorously reflected the character of the people and the land. Edward Hopper showed a new objectivity in depicting city and village. Thomas Benton, Charles Burchfield, John Steuart Curry, and Grant Wood had similar aims but differed in regional styles. Ben Shahn, on the other hand, turned his brush to social realism.

Inevitably, these painters of the recognizable forms of heartland America were challenged by a generation of abstract expressionists led by Jackson Pollock. Their movement to stress the painted surface both as a means of expression and as an end in itself opened the door for such innovators as Hans Hofmann, Willem de Kooning, and Josef Albers, and eventually for such curious movements as the op art and pop art of the 1960's.

209

The picture of Amelia Van Buren (above), done about 1891, exemplifies Thomas Eakins' mastery of portraiture. Eakins also turned to the world of action for subjects—the medical clinic, boxing, fishing —and had a gift for bringing the commonplace to life. John La Farge, who painted the water color of Samoa at top center was a student of light and shadow. He was a gifted muralist and a talented worker in stained glass.

Maurice Prendergast's water color of New York's Central Park (near left) was painted in 1895, when the artist was doing bright and gay street and holiday scenes. In 1914 he changed styles abruptly and afterward painted in a much more abstract manner. The painting above of Mr. and Mrs. Phelps Stokes is by John Singer Sargent, who gained an international reputation as a portrait painter. His other work, mainly murals, has not won such universal acclaim among critics.

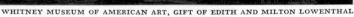

John Sloan called his early-twentieth-century painting of a New York elevated train (right) "Six o'Clock." Sloan was one of a group of eight artists dubbed the Ashcan School by their critics because they painted life as they saw it instead of choosing pretty subjects. Ben Shahn, who died only in 1969, devoted his artistic talent to supporting liberal causes. He first received wide praise in 1932 with a series called "The Passion of Sacco and Vanzetti," of which the above is one part. Edward Hopper, whose "Early Sunday Morning" (1930) is above right, painted America realistically, though he saw it as a lonely place.

212

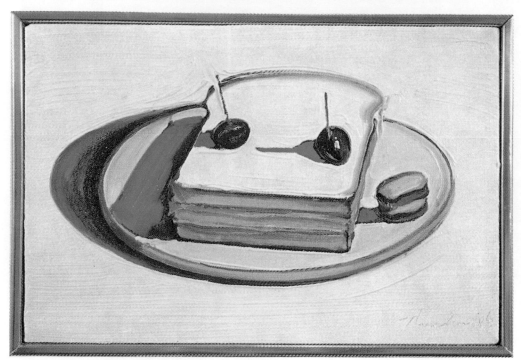

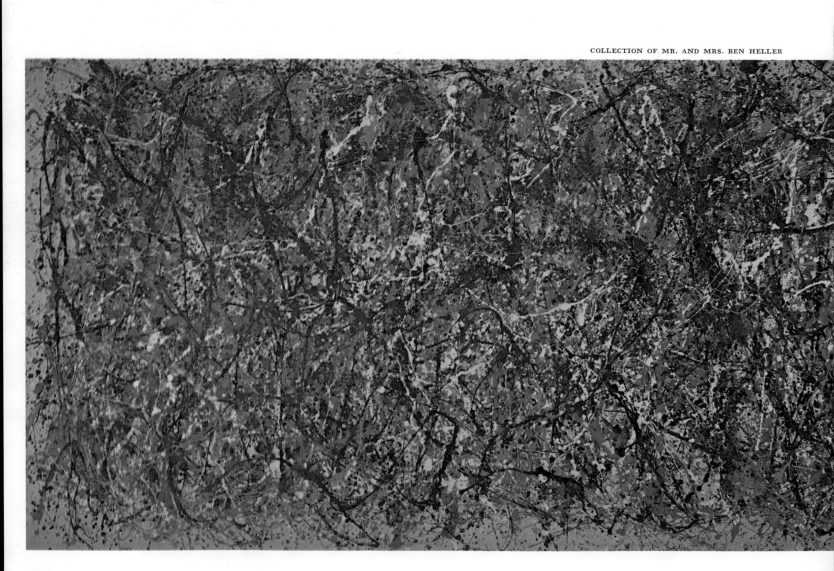

NATIONAL GALLERY, OSLO

Jackson Pollock titled the swirls of paint on canvas at lower left "One." Pollock, who died in an accident in 1956, was the leader of the abstract expressionist school—artists who expressed their inner feelings without the use of conventional symbols. "Sandwich," at top left, painted in 1963 by Wayne Thiebaud, is an example of pop art, which is difficult to define but takes as its subjects almost everything in mass culture, from paintings of soup cans to blow-ups of comic strips to painted plaster hot dogs. The painting of the boy, above, was made in Maine by Andrew Wyeth, who scorns the experimenters and follows the well-marked American tradition of treating simple subjects realistically and sympathetically.

William Glackens' "The Soda Fountain," painted in 1935, typifies hundreds of drugstores of the era. Sally Rand, opposite, famed fan dancer of the 1933 Century of Progress, changed to a bubble in 1934.

The Lean Years: 1930–39

The 1930's began under the cloud of the great stock market collapse; in fact, tremors from that event were still agitating Wall Street two months later when New Year's Day, 1930, arrived. In general, however, the country outwardly seemed pretty much as it had before the crash. Business and industry coasted along on their own momentum for a while, and people went on spending and buying as before. There was even a small bull market on Wall Street in the spring of 1930, which made investors hope that the economy was on the upturn, but by May the downward trend had resumed, and the Great Depression was settling over the land.

Security prices continued to fall lower until they reached bottom in the middle of 1932. During the same period many businesses faltered. Sales dropped off; the decreased demand for goods forced curtailment of production, with an accompanying cutting of salaries and wages and firing of workers. This in turn further reduced purchasing power, and so production was further reduced, more men were laid off—and the vicious circle went around and around. Unemployment, which had been one and a half million in 1929, tripled to four and a half million in 1930, reached eight million in 1931, twelve million in 1932, and almost thirteen million in 1933, the peak year, when one worker in four was unable to find a job. Other millions were underemployed, working perhaps three days a week or two weeks a month in order to spread the available work.

Those, however, are only statistics. In human terms, the depression meant hungry men in breadlines. It meant Chicago schoolteachers working without pay for months because the city had no money to pay them. It meant Iowa farmers defending their land against mortgage foreclosures by dragging judges from their benches and threatening to hang them. It meant homeless men riding the deadheads on every

$29⁹⁵ Cash Price COMPLETE

Think of it! A genuine Super Heterodyne —complete with all equipment—for less than $30. Exactly the same Set as the Consolette model described above, except for the cabinet. Convenient, new Mantel style walnut veneer cabinet. Only 13¾ by 8 by 17½ inches high.

217

1932's Peppiest Styles for Gay "HOT-SHOTS"

EVERYBODY GOES VARSITY $3.45
This trouser is neat and nifty in every detail from the 20-inch bottoms to the smoked pearl suspender buttons. Rakish lines, daringly emphasized by slash pockets on the sides, high waistband, two pockets in front, one for your smokes, the other for your ticker. Made of fine flannel over one-half wool. Pastel colors, of course.

freight train, always moving from one place to another in the eternal hope that somewhere there was work to be had. The depression meant a hundred different things to those caught in it, but for most families it meant doubling up, doing without, living in fear that the bread-winner would have another pay cut or, infinitely worse, lose his job.

Not everyone suffered to the same degree. Many people lived quite comfortably through the depression, but for the majority, even those who held on to their jobs through the worst of it, the depression was a constant presence. It hurt the middle-aged and the old most; they had lived their lives in the certitude that hard work would bring its reward in a comfortable and honored old age, and it was a bitter blow to see dreams shattered, jobs disintegrate, and savings disappear through no fault of their own. The young, more optimistic and re-silient, generally took events in stride and looked on the scrimping and the deprivations as inconveniences that would one day pass.

President Herbert Hoover, an intelligent man who had demonstrated his compassion by heading European relief after World War I, de-pended on the workings of orthodox economic theories to end the de-pression; his successor in 1933, Franklin Roosevelt, attempted to ac-complish the same thing by pump priming, deficit spending, and a rapid-fire series of actions meant to get various sectors of the economy off dead center. Roosevelt, with his initial burst of eggbeater activity, did cheer a dispirited country, and his Civil Works Administration, Works Progress Administration, Civilian Conservation Corps, and other alphabet agencies did put millions of unemployed to some kind of work, but it was only the approach of war at the end of the thirties that started the factory wheels turning at full speed again.

Not only economics but the climate itself seemed to conspire against man. In 1936 the Midwest experienced the coldest winter and hottest summer on record, and disastrous floods hit the Northeast. The next year the worst of all floods in American history rolled down the Ohio and Mississippi valleys. Much more far-reaching in its effect was the drought that afflicted the central part of the country from 1933 to 1937. Great Plains land, which never should have been plowed in the first place, became powder-dry and took to the air in great black bliz-zards that turned day into near-night and tinged the sky gray as far away as New York. Farmers, ruined by the drought, packed their few belongings into their jalopies and headed west, where they hoped some opportunity lay. These were the Okies—though they came from many Dust Bowl states besides Oklahoma—and their movement west was the greatest spontaneous migration in recent American history. As for the farms they left, the mortgage holders in many cases joined them together into large corporation farms, big businesses run on big-business principles. It was a trend that would spread across the coun-try; the day of the small family farm was on the wane.

The period provided one revealing insight into the stability of the American character. With so many unhappy unemployed, with busi-ness in trouble, the time seemed ripe for the overthrow of the capital-istic system promised by Marxist theory. Nothing of the sort happened.

218

There was some flirting with left-wing causes, but the Communist party gained very few members; most people kept their frustrations within the bounds of their allegiance to the Republican or Democratic parties.

Despite dark moods, the thirties were not a time of unrelieved doom and gloom. Professional baseball went on, college football teams strove as mightily as ever on Saturday afternoons in autumn (professional football had not yet acquired a large following), and there were high spirits and good fellowship at bars and taverns, for beer had been made legal in March, 1933, and in December of the same year the prohibition amendment was repealed. The Chicago Century of Progress, held in 1933 at the bottom of the depression, was a tremendous success. The supposedly disheartened American people came from all parts of the country to see the wonders of the time, including the Sky Ride, the marvels in the Hall of Science, and the exotic attractions of the midway, among them fan dancer Sally Rand. So successful was the fair that it was held over into 1934; in all, more than twenty million people attended, and at the closing the books showed a substantial profit.

The depression hit Broadway hard, but it did not dampen the creative vigor of playwrights and producers, for the thirties were privileged to see a number of memorable presentations. *Of Thee I Sing*, George Kaufman's musical comedy satire on presidential politics, appeared in 1932, and 1935 saw George Gershwin's *Porgy and Bess*, which has since become almost an American folk opera. As for drama, there were, to name only a few, *Green Pastures*, *Tobacco Road* (which subsequently ran for more than seven years), *The Barretts of Wimpole Street*, *Winterset*, *You Can't Take It With You*, *Our Town*, *High Tor*, *Of Mice and Men*, and *Abe Lincoln in Illinois*.

The theater, though, even with road companies, was available only to a comparative few. Motion pictures, on the other hand, were within reach of almost everyone except the most isolated and the most destitute (thirty-five cents was about the average admission charge for adults; children were admitted for fifteen or twenty-five cents). Escape was the pervading theme of films of the thirties; people with troubles of their own did not come out of an evening to watch the tribulations of others in dramas of social significance. The fantasies of Busby Berkeley were tremendously popular, musical extravaganzas like *Gold Diggers of 1933* and *42nd Street*, in which the plot—always about the unknown understudy who gets her chance to make good—was only an excuse for lavish production numbers featuring armies of long-legged girls marching down long staircases, forming geometric designs, or playing one hundred massed white pianos. Not all cinema was so exuberant, but most of it was removed from present reality in one way or another, with the offerings ranging from Mae West's *She Done Him Wrong* to *Lost Horizons* and *Little Caesar*, from the Marx brothers in *A Night at the Opera* to *Show Boat* and *The Wizard of Oz*.

It was radio, however, that was the universal entertainment, available to all at no cost. It is difficult for those who did not know radio

in its prime to conceive of it as creating an illusion of reality with its single dimension of sound, but skillful use of voice, sound effects, and music cues, together with the listener's imagination, built a three-dimensional feeling of actuality. Leading shows attracted tremendous audiences that were more enthralled than the television viewers of a later day. *Amos 'n' Andy,* an evening show, for instance, was so popular that some open-at-night department stores arranged to have it broadcast on their floors so that potential customers would not stay home to listen. A few of the other shows that once had large and loyal followings but now are only nostalgia-rousing names were *Stoopnagle and Bud, Lum and Abner, The National Barn Dance, Easy Aces, Fibber McGee and Molly, Singin' Sam,* and the shows featuring Fred Allen, Jack Benny, and Edgar Bergen with Charlie McCarthy.

The thirties were not much given to fads and crazes, but there were a few. In 1930 miniature golf swept the nation, and during the summer Americans spent a million dollars a day on thirty-five thousand courses, tapping golf balls through drainpipes and over and around other ingeniously contrived hazards. By the end of the next summer it was all over and the courses stood deserted. There was a resurgence of the marathon dancing of the twenties, and for a time it was a popular and inexpensive pastime to spend hours watching exhausted couples shamble endlessly around a cheerless arena. But the craze of all crazes was the ten-cent chain letter of 1935, which promised the person receiving it a return of $1,562.50 for the expenditure of a dime provided he (and a great many other persons) kept the chain unbroken. For a time so many chain letters were moving in the mail that the post office was overwhelmed. In Denver ninety additional clerks and carriers had to be hired to handle the extra load; in Des Moines, Iowa, banks were forced to send to the Federal Reserve Bank for more dimes. The lunacy began about March; by the middle of June it had run its course and was dead.

On a less frivolous level the 1930's can be marked as the beginning of the age of modern air travel. The precise year was 1933, when Boeing introduced its all-metal, ten-passenger 247. The plane's two engines were cowled to reduce air drag, and it could fly on one engine in an emergency. A few months later, still in 1933, almost before the industry had quite comprehended the full significance of the 247, which made obsolete all the wood-and-metal planes of the past, an even more advanced airplane went into service. Douglas delivered to Trans World Airlines twenty-five two-engine DC-2's, capable of carrying twelve passengers at 150 miles an hour, with a cruising range of one thousand miles. These were the first two of many increasingly sophisticated all-metal airliners; before the thirties were over American airlines were flying to Hong Kong in Asia and Portugal in Europe.

In November, 1934, the first all-steel diesel-powered passenger train went into regular main-line service. The diesels proved themselves not only more powerful but more versatile than steam locomotives for both freight and passenger service, and before long the smoke-puffing steamers with their mellow whistles began to disappear from the

American scene. The railroads upgraded their passenger service with streamlined modern trains that carried the newest and best in sleeping and dining accommodations, and toward the close of the thirties rail travel attained new standards of excellence.

As the 1930's ended, the airlines, which had carried only a handful of passengers in 1930, were hauling almost three million persons a year, and the automobile and intercity bus were making ever deeper inroads into travel that had once belonged to the railroads.

The thirties in some ways mark a transition period between traditional and modern medicine. In 1933 the first successful operation for removal of a lung for cancer was performed. As the decade ended, surgeons were beginning to work on the heart itself; in 1939 the first successful correction of a congenital heart defect was made. The first of the wonder drugs, sulfanilamide, was introduced in 1936 and was quickly superseded by a family of even more effective derivatives—sulfapyradine, sulfathiazole, sulfadiazine, and others—which proved remarkably potent against many infections, including pneumonia, peritonitis, scarlet fever, blood poisoning, gonorrhea, undulant fever, and impetigo, against which physicians had previously been almost helpless to do anything.

One drug whose benefits have been less clearly beneficial appeared during the mid-thirties when college students discovered that they could buy "pep pills" that enabled them to study the night through with a clear mind. Many of them learned, too, that after several days on the pills they collapsed in utter exhaustion. The pills were Benzedrine; they were the first of the family known as amphetamines, which in another twenty or thirty years would constitute a serious drug problem, with millions of capsules and tablets being taken each day by despondent housewives, weary businessmen, the bored of both sexes, and teen-agers seeking a thrill.

In the field of invention, the 1930's saw the development of radar (the British achieved theirs independently). Frequency modulation (FM) radio was invented in 1939, and nylon went into commercial production in 1938 in a very modest way: the public first saw it as toothbrush bristles, and not until the following year did the mills begin producing the yarns and threads that were to gladden female hearts.

During the thirties events abroad had posed dilemmas of decision for the American people. Most of them abhorred the dictatorships that had risen in Europe, and they sympathized with China in its unequal struggle against Japanese aggression. At the same time they were strongly isolationist; the First World War had been a disillusioning experience, and they had no desire to become involved overseas again.

Then, in the closing months of the thirties, Hitler's blitzkrieg tore through Europe. The United States was bound by law to follow a neutral course, but soon that neutrality would be eroded, bit by bit.

JOBLESS AND HUNGRY

The depression began settling on the nation in 1930. Its effect on any person during the next several years would depend on his financial resources or his ability to hold a job when those about him were losing theirs. At left is a bread line in New York's Bowery, a scene duplicated in almost every city of any size during the depths of the depression. At right an apple seller, symbol of this grim era, plies his curbside business. The two men below were photographed at Omaha, Nebraska, in 1938; both were past sixty years old and after years of unemployment had given up hope of ever finding work.

OVERLEAF: Nature added to man's woes with floods, drought, and dust storms. This windswept scene is in Swisher County, Texas, where soil once anchored by natural grass blew away when it was plowed and planted and drought came.

PHOTOWORLD

LIBRARY OF CONGRESS

THE DISPOSSESSED

During the drought years tens of thousands of farmers abandoned their homes, loaded their meager possessions onto battered cars, and headed west, where they hoped to find new opportunity. These dispossessed migrants came from all parts of the drought-stricken plains, but the exodus was greatest from the Dust Bowl, where they left behind farmsteads half-buried in drifted soil, like the Oklahoma farm above. The woman and child at right were photographed while on their way west.

MIGRANTS ADRIFT

California was the promised land to the Okies, where they expected to find work and a new life. Instead, wages were low, jobs scarce, and they were barred from many communities by vigilante bands. The elderly woman at top left was living in a squatters' camp on the outskirts of Bakersfield in 1936. The women with songbooks at bottom left are at a mothers' club meeting in California's Kern County. The family above are living in a tent; their weary and dejected expressions reveal eloquently that they have not found their dream in the golden West.

OVERLEAF: This is Times Square on election night, 1932. Though Roosevelt would hearten a dispirited nation, he would not be able to end the depression.

Roosevelt's Civil Works Administration was designed to put men to work as quickly as possible; it gave jobs to four million men on highways and projects like the one above. The National Recovery Act—later struck down by the Supreme Court—was meant to raise prices through voluntary agreements regulating competition among industries; the young ladies at upper right show their support by painting the NRA emblem on their backs so the sun can stencil it there. The Works Progress Administration put jobless to work at everything from airport construction to mural painting; the project below hired jobless music teachers. The Civilian Conservation Corps gave youths fresh-air work helping conserve natural resources; the young men at lower right are in a training camp.

A NIGHT ON THE TOWN

Despite the depression, the thirties were not a joyless decade, especially for the young, and a night out was not necessarily expensive. It was the era of the big bands—of Paul Whiteman, Ben Bernie, Glen Miller, Woodie Herman, the Dorsey brothers, and others now only legends—and for the great majority unable to dance to live music there were taverns with juke boxes and beer for a nickel a glass and good companions. The couple at right are making the most of a Saturday night out in Clarksdale, Mississippi, in 1939. The trio above are socialites enjoying to the utmost the entertainment at a Manhattan supper club.

OVERLEAF: This vista of well-dressed and prosperous-looking humans is the Starlight Roof, New York's most popular rendezvous for dining and dancing in 1934, one of the bottom years of the depression.

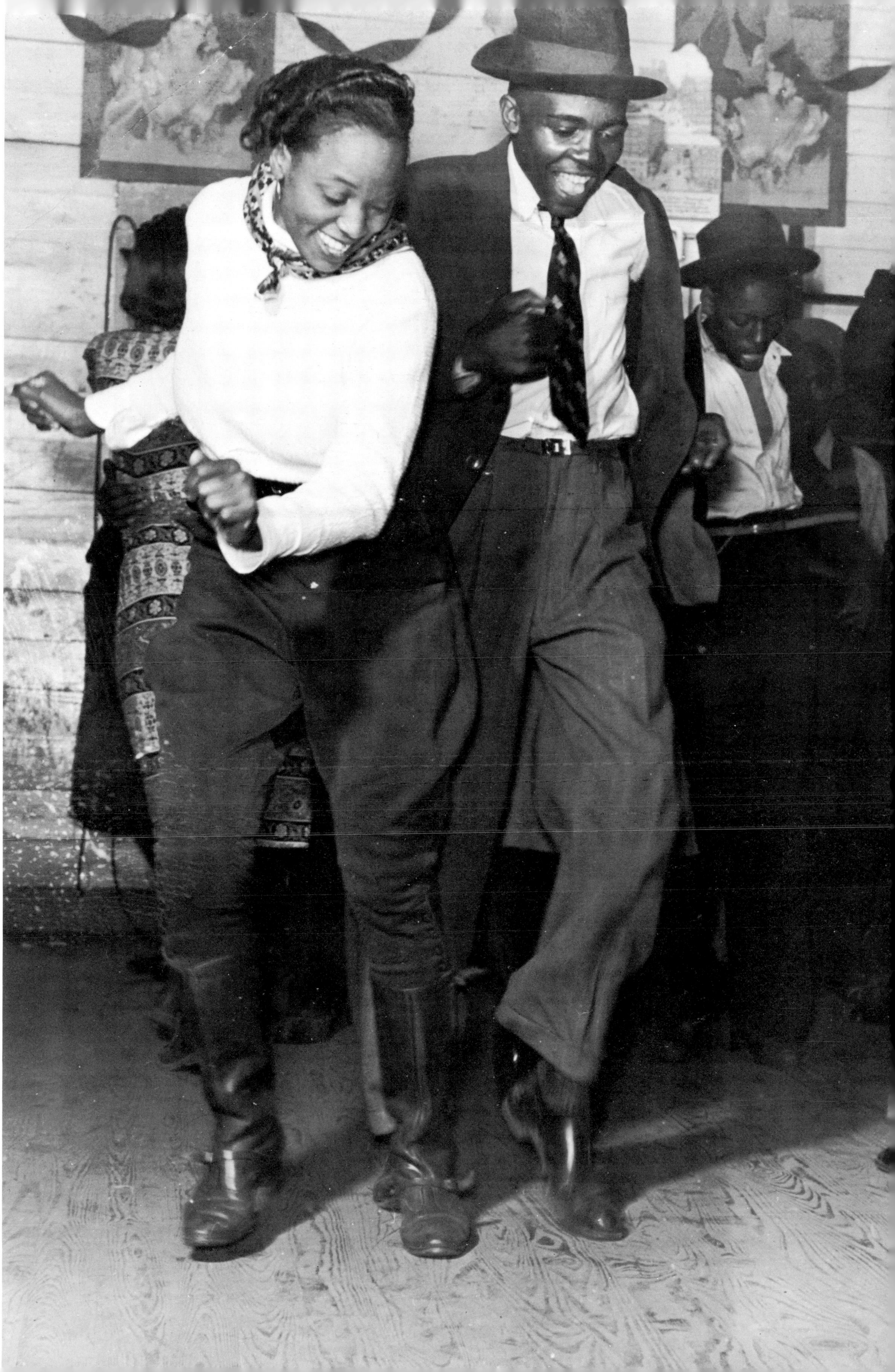

LIBRARY OF CONGRESS

TWO FACES OF LEARNING

In spite of the best efforts of well-intentioned men and women, opportunities are not always equal for everyone, and as the two photographs on these pages show, one inequity is in the field of education. The confident young women at the right are students at Wellesley, one of the nation's better colleges for women. The day is May 1, 1936; freshmen (in white) march to chapel between seniors fresh from their sunrise hooprolling contest, an annual May Day rite. Tradition has it that the winner will be the first married. Above, in a much less festive setting, a woman attempts to share her own small store of learning with two small pupils. The lesson she has chalked on the blackboard reads, "The rain are fallin."

238

COLLECTION OF FRED TRUMP, JR.

One man's fun and recreation may well cause another to shudder. For many years New Yorkers have been jamming themselves together on Coney Island beaches in an intimacy that a sardine might resent, and apparently enjoying it immensely. The tangle at left is a Fourth of July crowd in 1935. Above is another aspect of Coney Island: the popular—among spectators—air jet in the old Steeplechase Park catches a victim. The date: 1932.

OVERLEAF: In a quieter mood, as a countryman's pleasures usually are, parents and friends look on as 4-H members prepare their sheep for judging at a county fair in Kansas.

GRANT HEILMAN

WORKERS AND BUILDERS

During the depression most large constructon projects were curtailed, except for those such as Boulder Dam and TVA that were funded by the government's public works program. A notable exception was New York's Rockefeller Center, under construction at left, where eleven buildings went up between 1931 and 1940. Above, a crew at the shops of the Reading Railroad in Pennsylvania works on locomotive maintenance, necessary no matter how hard the times.

OVERLEAF: Unsung heroes of the depression were small businesses, such as the neighborhood grocery, that were able to survive the buffetings of the era.

O'ER THE RAMPARTS WE WATCH

UNITED STATES
ARMY AIR FORCES

Above is a wartime recruiting poster for the Army Air Forces. The world entered the nuclear age during the 1940's; at top right is a photograph of one of the 1946 atomic bomb tests at Bikini atoll.

WAR and Change: 1940–49

For Americans, the foreign scene was a grim and shocking one during the first months of the 1940's. Little Finland had been beaten into submission by Russia. Denmark and Norway had been seized by Hitler; the Low Countries had been shattered by Nazi blitzkrieg; and France had collapsed before the end of June, leaving only Great Britain to oppose Hitler's conquest of all western Europe. In Asia, Japanese forces continued to ravage China.

Americans were not only stunned but confused. The spirit of isolationism was strong through the nation, but with each somber new development the feeling grew that something should be done, especially to help England. There was wide disagreement on how deeply we should get involved, and a great debate went on, often violent and acrimonious, with the Committee to Defend America by Aiding the Allies as the loudest spokesman for giving all possible aid short of war, and the America First Committee as the vehement voice of isolationism. The United States began building its own defenses, initiated its first peacetime draft, and as public opinion gradually swung in favor of aid, began sending help to Britain in increasing quantities. Then the Japanese attacked Pearl Harbor on December 7, 1941, and ended all debate. (Germany and Italy declared war on the United States soon thereafter.) The next morning there were long lines of young men at recruiting stations waiting to volunteer, and the nation, confused but determined, was beginning the tremendous task of transforming itself into a fighting machine.

(P) HANDSOME BROWN AND WHITE HALF BROGUE with a straight medallion tip . . . another Summertime favorite. Heavy perforations add to the substantial, well-made appearance of this popular style.

24 A 6286—Brown and White Leather. Ship. wt. 2 lbs. 10 oz. *State size*........ 7.98

249

*Pure Silk Crepes
at 16.98*

To fight a war that extended over much of the globe, the armed services eventually put into uniform more than sixteen million volunteers and draftees. The military campaigns in which they took part must be related in another kind of history, but the tremendous effort of training, arming, transporting, and sustaining this host of men and women in uniform transformed the home front. For one thing, it put an emphatic end to the depression. In 1940 there were still more than eight million unemployed; the next year, as the nation began putting its defenses in order, the figure dropped to five and a half million. In 1942, under the spur of actual war, it was down to two and a half million, and by 1944 it was only 670,000, a rock-bottom figure since it would just about account for the number of workers normally between jobs when the count was made.

As for industry, it performed prodigies of production. During the depression, when efficiency and economy were the price of survival in most businesses, output per man-hour had increased an estimated 41 per cent compared with 21 per cent in the 1920's. With the coming of war, industry was able to make the utmost use of its increased efficiency. The producer of war materials did not have to worry about overproduction or excessive costs; the one demand made of him was that he turn out as much as possible in as short a time as possible. The government paid the bill. Automobile makers began making airplanes and tanks; a maker of hydraulic pumps was soon turning out antiaircraft guns; a company that had made ladies' compacts was able to make the conversion to producing parts for shell fuzes.

Never before had the nation been so much on the move. The trains that shuttled across the land were filled with men in uniform. Most also carried a contingent of young women, off to spend some last weeks near a husband in the service in spite of government warnings that living accommodations near military bases were meager or nonexistent. The buses were loaded to capacity with Georgia sharecroppers, Ozark hillbillies, Dakota plowboys, for jobs were easy to get and paid well, even for men with no experience. The Census Bureau estimated in 1945 that more than fifteen million Americans were living in counties other than those they had been in at the time of Pearl Harbor; almost eight million of these were in different states, and more than three and a half million in a different part of the country.

Because there was nowhere near enough manpower to fill all needs, the nation drew heavily on its womanpower. The armed services all enlisted women—the WAC's, WAVES, SPAR's, and women Marines— and by 1945 well over a quarter of a million women were in uniform, many in specialized jobs such as air control tower operators, code room clerks, aviation mechanics, and technicians of many kinds. Their influx into industry was even more spectacular. Rosie the Riveter, they were called, and many were just that, and were often handier than men at their jobs because, being smaller, they could more easily crawl with their riveting hammers into cramped spaces such as the wings of bombing planes. They did other things too: welding, grinding lenses, making parachutes, maintaining locomotives, ferrying airplanes, just about anything that did not depend on brute strength—and a few things that did.

The American people had to tighten their belts, but it was far from total war on the home front. Almost a year passed before the government took the unpopular step of rationing gasoline. In the spring of 1942 food rationing began, starting with sugar, until eventually all meat and canned goods were on the list, and so were shoes, coal, fuel oil, and gasoline. Many items not rationed were in short supply because they used strategic materials; thus it was difficult to buy bobby pins or nylon hosiery, alarm clocks or razor blades. A patriotic housewife saved her tin cans for the scrap drive (first cleaning them, removing the ends, and flattening them), saved her bacon drippings and other grease (for explosives), saved old aluminum and various other materials. Most families stretched their ration points with a Victory garden and home canning. If they bought toothpaste or anything else in a collapsible metal tube, they had to turn in an old tube in exchange.

Despite the annoying shortages, no one went hungry and there was the greatest prosperity in years. But it was a somber prosperity. The absence of so many sons, brothers, husbands, sweethearts, and friends, and the casualty lists, were constant reminders that a very real and cruel war was being waged, and most citizens responded by working hard and by making the sacrifices asked of them.

At last, in August of 1945, it was finished—but things did not return to the way they had been. America soon found that the world had only exchanged one set of would-be dictators for another. By 1947 Russia, our brave wartime ally, had become an antagonist, and the Cold War was on. Bankrupt western Europe was rescued by the Marshall Plan, Greece and Turkey were saved from Communism by the Truman Doctrine, a heroic airlift kept Berlin out of Russian hands. Like it or not, America was deeply involved in world affairs.

The war was not followed by the postwar depression that ordinarily follows wars. The factories kept humming to fill the tremendous pent-up demand by a long-deprived people who wanted to buy automobiles, toasters, washing machines, refrigerators, and countless other items that had long been unobtainable. Inflation, however, skimmed much of the cream from the soaring postwar economy as round after round of wage and price increases raised the cost of almost everything that went into the cost of living. As a result of the scramble for scarce goods, a black market in many items developed: for a time the only people eating steak were the wealthy or personal friends of the butcher's.

Within a year after the end of the war some ten million men and women had been returned from military to civilian life fairly smoothly, thanks to a flourishing economy and the cushioning effects of terminal pay. Then an interesting phenomenon occurred. The marriage rate in 1946 soared to the highest point in American history. The birth rate began to climb that same year, and in 1947 reached an all-time peak, though it was to remain high through the rest of the 1940's and the 1950's. It might also be noted that the divorce rate in 1946 set a record;

Dresser and Mirror $63.50

DRESSER AND MIRROR: Top 47¾ by 20⅞ in. Base height 35 in. 4 drawers. Top drawer looks like 3 drawers. Hanging Plate Glass Mirror 43⅞ by 28⅜ in. overall. Enameled pin tray in top drawer. One drawer has removable divider for shirts. Shipping weight 200 lbs........$63.50

MODERNIZE YOUR BARN

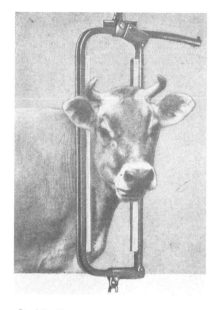

Good Quality. A well-made Stanchion priced exceptionally low. Full weight, durable materials used throughout. Single hinged uprights are 1⅝ by ⅞ by 3/16-in. high carbon steel U-bars. Guided by U-bar steel slide and held by positive, cowproof lock. Only one hand required to open; simply grasp top of stanchion and press down on latch with the thumb. You don't have to set down your pail of milk to release cow.

87 B 4773M—Lined Stanchion. Each.....$2.19
For 10 or more. Each..................2.09

a good many of the break-ups were young couples who had married in the emotional atmosphere of wartime and had found when the husband returned from overseas that they were complete strangers with virtually nothing in common.

One effect of the flood of postwar marriages was an acute housing shortage. There were incidents of young couples sleeping in bus stations or on park benches, though most managed to make do by moving in with their parents. The construction industry worked feverishly putting up endless rows of houses on countless acres of land. As with any enterprise that promises quick profits, unqualified and unscrupulous operators moved into the field, and there were complaints of collapsing foundations, warping from the use of green lumber, improperly installed sewage systems, and other gross incompetences, but on the average the builders probably did as well as could have been expected in a near-emergency situation.

Another phenomenon of the times was the invasion of colleges by returned veterans, whose education was made possible by the liberal GI Bill of Rights. The veterans gave campuses a different look, especially since many of them had wives and often babies. They were older and more serious than most of their fellow students just out of high school, and they were disdainful of many traditional features of the college scene that they considered irrelevant in a changed world. It was their scorn of Greek letter societies that gave fraternities a blow from which they have not yet recovered on many campuses.

Stepped-up wartime research had added many new items and procedures to the arsenal of medicine. Revolutionary surgical techniques were developed or refined under the terrible urgency of the battlefield. Penicillin, though discovered in 1929, had not been tried on a human being until 1941, and then came into its own as mass production methods were developed. The first three antibiotics—streptomycin, Chloromycetin, and Aureomycin—were discovered during the forties, and the first antihistamine, benedril, was discovered in 1943 and was followed by a number of others effective against allergies and in one case, Dramamine, against motion sickness. Nevertheless, there was some concern about the state of the nation's health. It was revealed that 72 per cent of the young men called for the peacetime draft in the nation's ten largest cities were being rejected for physical or mental disabilities; in New York City the rate was 87.5 per cent.

The forties saw the beginning of television. Commercial televising was all ready to go in 1941 when the war cut it off. So, when peace returned and production was resumed, television had had time for further development; it was in a much more advanced state than radio had been in its infancy and was all set to entertain the first video generation with small-screen versions of Milton Berle, *Howdy Doody, Queen for a Day,* roller derbies, and Thursday night wrestling.

Women's fashions contributed their small bit to the story of the forties, as they do to every period. During the first part of the decade skirts reached a bit below the knee, and no one was especially unhappy. Then in 1947 designers decreed the "New Look," with hemlines dropping somewhere to the vicinity of mid-calf, and there was an anguished outcry from thousands of women, especially those with good legs. A group of Texas women even organized a Just an Inch Below the Knee Club in a fight to keep hems from dropping too far, and the club spread briefly across the nation. The effort was futile, though a future day would come when not the knee but the thigh would be the limit. Speaking of legs, 1946 was the year of nylon queues. During the war sheer hosiery had been off the market, for both nylon and rayon were strategic materials. Most women, rather than wear thick lisle stockings, went barelegged, sometimes using leg makeup as a substitute for hosiery. When nylon hosiery again began to appear on the market, there were crowds of women standing in line before opening time whenever a store announced that it would have the precious items on sale, and scenes of near-riot often occurred.

For once, farmers were enjoying postwar prosperity as much as everyone else. And life down on the farm was not what it once had been. The horse was giving way to the tractor, the milking machine was replacing the ancient hand grip-and-squeeze method, and machinery was doing what muscle had once done in the hayfield, at corn-husking time, in the feed lot. By the end of the 1940's 85 per cent of all farms were electrified (in 1935, when the Rural Electrification Administration came into being, only about 10 per cent of farms had electricity). As a result, the lot of the farmer's wife was changed as drastically as was that of her husband. The farm kitchen was equipped with electric refrigerator, mixer, toaster, iron, washer, and other appliances; the wood-burning range had been replaced by an electric stove, and the farm wife's proverbial life of drudgery had been exchanged for a routine not too different from that of her city sister.

Probably the single most significant event of the 1940's was the freeing of the power that is locked in the nucleus of the atom. The peaceful uses of atomic energy have the potential for bringing a brighter future to the human race, but it is the destructive power of the atom that weighs on the minds of men. Americans have had to face the fact that for the first time in their history isolation is impossible; there is no longer any place to hide. The earth has become a very small vessel, and we are all passengers in it together.

KEEP OUR BOYS HOME

During the uneasy days of 1940 and 1941, when most of western Europe was falling to Hitler, many Americans felt that the struggle was none of our business, not even to the extent of giving economic aid. Though sentiment slowly swung toward aiding the Allies, isolationist spirit remained so strong that in August, 1941, less than four months before Pearl Harbor, an act to extend the draft passed the House of Representatives by a single vote, 203 to 202. The ladies at the left kneeling in prayer are members of the "Mothers' Crusade" in Washington to lobby against passage of the Lend-Lease Bill to provide aid to friendly nations—chiefly Britain. The bill was approved despite their opposition.

GOOD-BY, DEPRESSION

The shadow of war finally ended the depression as the nation entered the 1940's. Many factories were operating for the first time in years as the United States not only began rearming but sent an increasing amount of aid abroad. The "No Help Needed" signs were disappearing, and cash registers were jingling again. The group above having a late lunch and beer in a Chicago taven in 1941 are well dressed and obviously have money in their pockets, yet during the depression blacks in general suffered far greater unemployment than did whites. The hilly, muddy street at right is in Pittsburgh; to residents this 1941 view was beautiful because the mills in the background were once again putting out smoke—and smoke meant jobs.

256

IT WASN'T ALL CHEERING

Pearl Harbor came, and there was no more argument about whether or not America should be involved in the affairs of Europe and Asia. Amid all the frenetic activity of converting a great industrial nation to a wartime basis, the conflict, like all others in history, remained highly personal to the individual men and women caught up in it. The most repeated and poignant of all vignettes throughout the entire war was the one above, a serviceman saying good-by to his girl. At right, a sailor on leave catches a nap in a convenient lobby. A great many young men in uniform and away from home for the first time found that the most painful burdens they bore in serving their country were homesickness and loneliness.

258

World War II was the first conflict to see large numbers of women in uniform; above, WAC recruits draw their clothing issue. Below, soldiers on a train trip pass the time with a deck of cards. In the wartime insecurity, when men often left suddenly for far places, many couples plunged into marriage, and weddings like the one at right with a bridegroom in uniform were common.

The demand of war industries for workers was voracious, yet the armed forces were taking millions of men out of the labor market. Women filled the gap; there were more than nineteen million of them employed in 1944, up 30 per cent from 1941. At right, a lady welder competently handles what had been strictly a man's job. Above, an almost completely female crew makes barrage balloons. On the domestic front, below, a Victory gardener sprays her vegetables with an insect killer.

OVERLEAF: *There had been dancing in the streets, kissing of strangers, and other jubilating on May 8, 1945, the day Germany surrendered, but there had been the sobering realization that there was still a war to be won in the Pacific. No such reservations dampened the celebrations in August when Japan gave up. This happy scene is in San Francisco on V-J Day, the day Japan surrendered.*

263

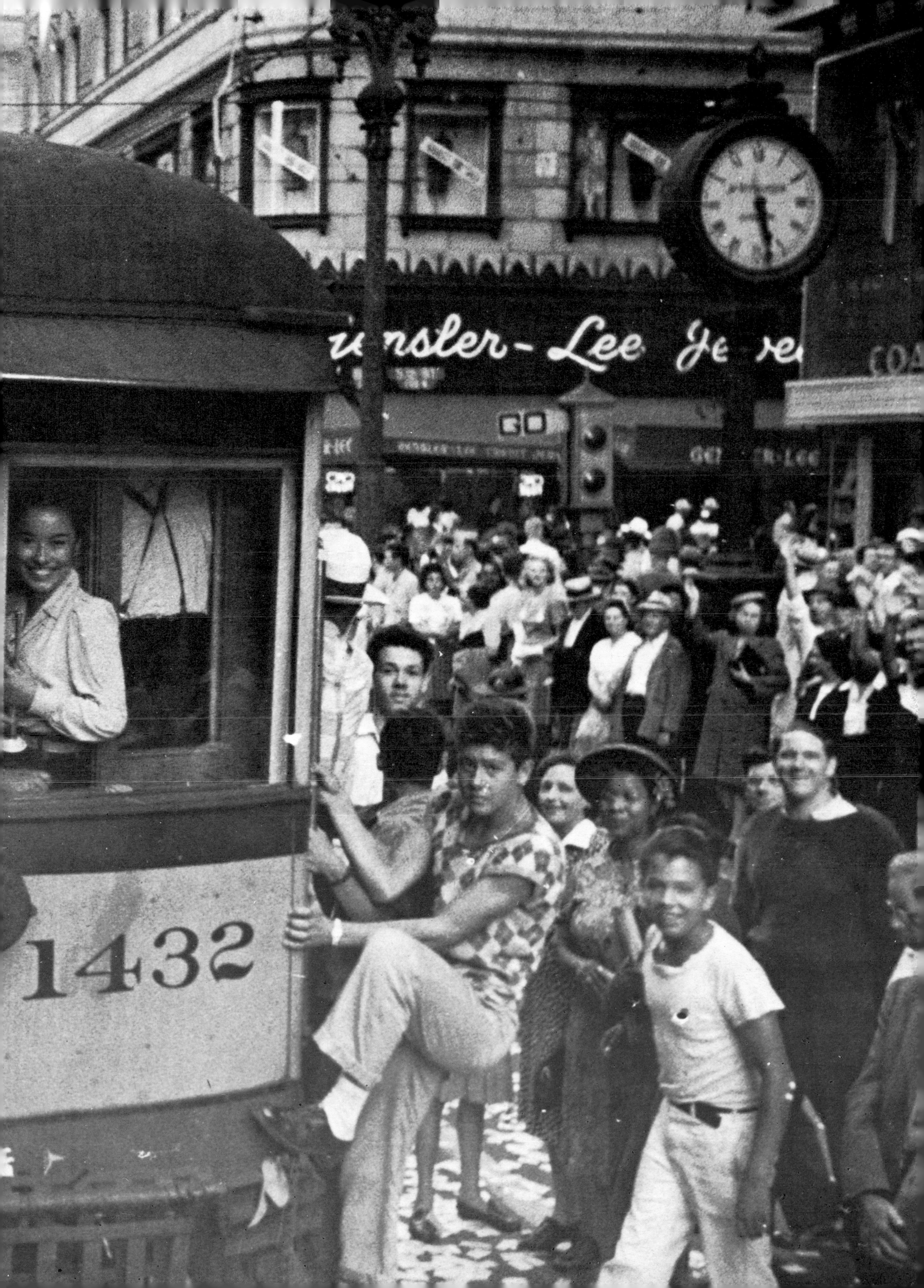
1432

THE POSTWAR WORLD

The postwar world had its problems and its innovations. Most shortages were overcome as factories reconverted to peacetime production, but housing would remain in short supply for many years. The carpenters at top right are erecting a prefab house; it was a technique that helped very little to solve the housing shortage. Television was new on the scene: some mothers blessed it as a built-in baby sitter; others feared it would turn their children into mindless zombies. College campuses took on a new look as veterans, many of them married, returned to classrooms with GI Bill help. The young family at right is at Dartmouth in 1945.

266

ON A QUIETER NOTE

In spite of postwar shortages and cold war tensions, the American people found it easy to settle back again into their everyday peacetime ways of life. The steamy scene above is a New England clambake; the place is Boothbay, Maine, in 1947. The pair at right is at a country auction north of Boston; the gentleman has already bid successfully on two antique lanterns.

Some things were little touched by time and change. In the forties these hill folk in Cumberland,

Kentucky, still followed the old-time religion and went down to the river to baptize.

WIDE WORLD

TEEN-AGE ANTICS

The young in every generation must be served. Teen-age girls found their special hero in a skinny young man named Frank Sinatra; the three rapt maidens above are watching one of the singer's early performances in 1943. Shrieking, weeping, and swooning were the usual responses at such events. Such irrational behavior overcame the young of both sexes when Harry James and his orchestra played at the Paramount in New York; the transported audience jitterbugged in the aisles and even on the stage. The exhausted couple at the right are finishing their jitterbug turn during a dance contest in New York's Central Park. Actually, it was found that the favorite dance during the 1940's was the reliable old foxtrot.

CONCERNING FASHIONS

Some women liked the longer "New Look" styles of 1947; some did not. The young New York secretary above was one who did; she was quoted as saying that the longer skirts were flattering to most figures. The girls at right with their off-the-shoulder blouses, rolled jeans, and flats are wearing leisure dress that definitely was not flattering to most figures. Fortunately, the style was short-lived.

274

Because old handicrafts have been largely replaced by machine work, this picture of Michigan farm women working on a patchwork quilt, though taken in the 1940's, resembles an old album photo.

OVERLEAF: *The small, unmechanized farm, too, was fast becoming an anachronism in the forties, out of place in a modern world. This one is in the Blue Ridge Mountains, near Boone, North Carolina.*

Today's population trends are toward cities and suburbia; this photo of Los Angeles foreshadows a day when some city dwellers may never see the country. At right, visual pollution by roadside signs.

The Changing Landscape

Mankind, for better or for worse, has acquired the ability to change the face of the earth on which he lives. Even within the memory of living men this capacity to alter radically the environment has been increased manyfold. Scarcely more than a generation ago the laborer with a shovel and wheelbarrow was an essential part of every construction project, and the horse was called on to pull and haul. Now human and animal muscle have been superseded by an array of giant machines for moving earth, drilling rock, lifting huge loads, and performing almost every other specialized task. With their aid today's engineer can gouge away hills, divert streams, drain swamps, create lakes, lay down networks of superhighways, erect buildings hundreds of feet high.

Nowhere has this mastery over environment been exerted more extensively than in the United States. The results have been the wonder of the world, and they have contributed to the high American standard of living. But they have not been an unmixed blessing, and there have been serious doubts as to whether or not some of the results are worth the price. The highways that enable one to travel easily and swiftly from place to place have often been built with insolent disregard for the communities they traverse. Cities, in providing growing populations with the amenities of modern living, have polluted air and water. Strip miners, uprooting the land in their search for coal, have desolated great areas of once-lovely Appalachian mountain country. Automobile graveyards blight the countryside; urban sprawl has become an accepted part of the landscape.

The malignant effects of growth are not inevitable. Strong forces within science, industry, and the public are working to divorce ugliness from development and pollution from progress. They come none too soon: our store of green earth, fresh air, and clean water is dwindling fast.

When William Wall made his somewhat idealized painting of Homestead, Pennsylvania (above), in the 1880's, he and many other Americans still hoped for a happy marriage of industry and rural countryside, in which workers could go from mill or factory to neat, white-painted village homes only a short distance away. It did not work out that way; most factory towns became grimy, smoke-shrouded places. But today the old dream is being realized in many places as clean, nonpolluting —and often carefully landscaped—industries move out into the suburbs or even into communities far from large cities. At lower right is a section of the long-abandoned Chesapeake and Ohio Canal, begun in 1828. Although a major engineering feat of its day, it shows how little impact the best technology of its time could make on the landscape. At right above is Thomas Benton's "Boom Town, 1928," about the oil seekers of the 1920's, a time when America was just beginning to realize that tremendous amounts of fuel were needed to power the automobile age.

ROCHESTER MEMORIAL ART GALLERY

A. AUBREY BODINE

The demands of a growing population have turned great areas of farm and woodland into miles of urban sprawl and acres of look-alike houses—but not always. Developers with imagination have created many attractive neighborhoods, such as the Paterson, New Jersey, development above, with its curving streets and houses of varied architecture. At left is Hoover Dam, on the Colorado River; such structures have changed the character of entire regions, not only by the lakes they have created, but, mainly in the West, by turning deserts into farmland through irrigation. At the right a "fish-eye" camera lens emphasizes the impact of the automobile on the environment; the picture shows a freeway exchange in Los Angeles. The federal highway program begun in the 1950's has sent superhighways weaving a web across the country, through cities and countryside, through woods and over rivers.

HERBERT LOEBEL

NATIONAL PARK SERVICE

Among the uglier scars on today's landscape are automobile graveyards (left); one cannot escape them even in rural regions. Below is proof that a city's waterfront need not be unsightly. Chicago's Grant Park was kept free of commerce and industry as a result of a twenty-year legal battle waged by Aaron Montgomery Ward. Above is a different kind of recreation area, one that is unique in a nation where open space is more and more at a premium. The picture is of the Boundary Waters Canoe Area of northern Minnesota and adjoining Canada, a maze of lakes and forest where one travels only by canoe—all motors are forbidden.

STEPHANIE DINKINS

Prosperity and Problems: 1950-59

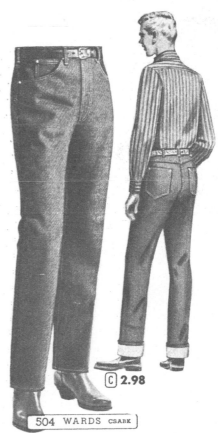

(C) 2.98

504 WARDS CSABK

WESTERN MADE SADDLE PANTS

ONLY $2⁸⁹ EA. IN LOTS OF 3

[C] **Powr-House Better Quality.** 13¾-oz. White-back Blue Denim Sanforized for extra wear. Genuine Western form-fit without bind. Tapered legs, low rise and most features of "A" above but not specially guaranteed, no extra hip seam.

The 1950's have sometimes been called the Bland Decade or the Complacent Decade, because the era was supposedly one when nothing much happened and everyone played it safe. These are unfortunate and misleading labels. The fifties had their own special character, but far from being bland, the period had its share of troubles, turmoil, and uncertainties.

Economically it was a good time for the United States. Business was healthy, production was up, people were buying. There was rather a sharp recession in 1957–58, but the nation coasted through it without serious consequences. Almost all the statistics told the same story. The gross national product, that annual measure of America's economic progress, was $318 billion in 1950; it climbed steadily to $428 billion in 1959. There were some forty-nine million motor vehicles on the highways in 1950; ten years later there were well over seventy-one million. People had more time and money for recreation: the number of hunting and fishing licenses sold between 1950 and 1959 increased 40 per cent; the value of outboard motors sold in the same period went up almost 50 per cent; the number of bowling teams grew by 120 per cent. Average family income climbed steadily during the decade.

Yet this picture of a prosperous and contented nation was flawed. To begin with, the fifties were only half a year old when in June, 1950, the United States found itself at war again, fighting to defend South

OVERALLS, SIZES 1-5

[G] For boys or girls. Buckle suspenders adjust., snap fastener sides; elastic back. Wash alone. *Sizes:* 1, 2, 3, 4, 5. Ship. wt. ea. 8 oz. STURDY 6-OZ. WT. BLUE DENIM. *State size.*
31B3547—Each 1.19; 2 for 2.35

SUPREME GAS RANGE 187.50

[A] WARDS SUPREME GAS RANGE offers quality cooking performance and convenient extra features that save time and work.

Korea from invasion. At first the American public applauded the action of President Truman in resisting aggression by Communist North Korea, but when the war settled down to stalemate, the national mood began to sour. When former President Herbert Hoover urged total withdrawal from both Asia and Europe, and a return to the isolationism concept of Fortress America, there were many who agreed with him.

The magnitude of Dwight D. Eisenhower's victory in the presidential election of 1952 said something about the mood of the American people. They were weary of problems and emergencies and sacrifices. They had survived the long, lean years of depression only to see them followed by a global war; victory in that conflict had been frustrated by the Cold War; Western Europe had had to be rescued from chaos, and billions of dollars in foreign aid had been sent abroad year after year. And now the war in Korea. People were exhausted emotionally and mentally. When Eisenhower appeared with his broad grin and avuncular manner, the reaction of millions was to quit worrying about the state of the world and turn matters over to the general who had managed the war in Europe so capably.

The inauguration of President Eisenhower did not, however, usher in the period of national unity and general good feeling for which most Americans longed. When the Democrats were still in power there had been accusations that Communists and their sympathizers were infiltrating the government, and a handful of fellow travelers had actually been uncovered. The hubbub would likely have subsided had not Senator Joseph McCarthy of Wisconsin discovered that there was political pay dirt in exploiting the treason charge, and he ruthlessly and cynically embarked on a course of character assassination. The inauguration of a Republican President did not slow McCarthy at all; during televised congressional hearings he made unsupported charges against public servants of unquestioned loyalty and rectitude with complete recklessness. Only when he was censured by the Senate in 1954 was he silenced, but by then the witch hunt he had begun was moving of its own momentum. Not only government employees but scientists, teachers, actors, television personalities, writers, even clergymen, lost jobs and reputations because of accusations made by unknown informers. The rule that a man was innocent till proved guilty was replaced by one that considered him guilty until he could prove that he was innocent. McCarthyism endured long after the senator had passed from the picture, ruining reputations and setting neighbor against neighbor.

The 1950's gained their label, the Bland or Complacent Decade, mainly because of the willingness of the youth of the time to accept the status quo. College years are ordinarily a time of intellectual ferment, when radical ideas and idealistic causes are fervently espoused —and forgotten two or three years later. But the college generation of the fifties declined to get excited. It was said of the typical college student of the time that his total life plan was to go to work after graduation for a good company where he could be secure until retire-

290

ment, marry the right girl, move to a comfortable home in a respectable suburb, and join the country club. In college his youthful urges to kick over the traces expressed themselves in such odd ways as swallowing goldfish, trying to cram as many students as possible into restricted spaces like sports cars and telephone booths, and in the spring, when the mating urge became irresistible, making pantie raids on the women's dormitories. Like all generalizations, this one is too pat and all-inclusive, but by and large the equable student of the fifties was a different person from his predecessors, and certainly from those who would follow him in the 1960's.

The behavior of the college generation of the fifties is probably explainable in terms of the world it lived in. Instead of dreaming about founding their own businesses, many young men prepared themselves for futures as corporation executives. Corporate giants had come to dominate the American economic scene. By 1956, 135 corporations were said to own 45 per cent of the industrial assets of the United States; a good part of the remainder was owned by corporations that were very large by most standards. The self-made man without a college education was a vanishing breed; the turn-of-the-century days when leaders of industry intoned that a man who went to college would lose four precious years when he should be learning a business were long past; instead recruiters now came to colleges to seek out bright young graduates who would fit into their expanding corporate structures.

Meanwhile, technological developments were rapidly changing the character of most industries. Machines guided by complex electronic circuitry proved capable of performing complete sequences of operations. Computers had made their appearance during World War II, but they were enormously clumsy by today's standards, and they were custom-built. In 1954 the first commercial UNIVAC (Universal Automatic Computer) was sold, and another industrial revolution had begun. Computers became more and more versatile and sophisticated in their ability to handle the drudgery of such chores as bookkeeping, billing, inventory, and the like. There were inevitably some men and women thrown out of work by automation and computers—as harness and buggy makers had once been displaced by the automobile—but new industries such as electronics took up the slack, and total employment and wages rose steadily.

Negroes made an important step forward in their fight for equality when the Supreme Court ruled in 1954 that "separate but equal" schools violated the guarantees of the Fourteenth Amendment. The decision overturned in part at least the famous *Plessy v. Ferguson* ruling of 1896, which held that segregation was not discrimination as long as Negroes were provided facilities equal to those of whites. In 1954 Chief Justice Earl Warren delivered the unanimous opinion of the Court, which said, "We conclude that in the field of public education the doctrine of 'separate but equal' has no place. Separate educational facilities are inherently unequal."

Some border states acted almost immediately to integrate their

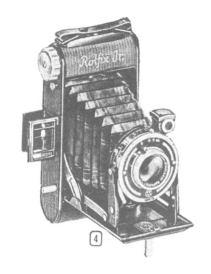

FOLDING CAMERAS

Portis Hats,

Smooth-Running Portables $48.50

schools; most Southern states used one stratagem after another for years to frustrate the ruling, and it is far from completely implemented yet. Blacks moved for equal rights on another front when they demonstrated against segregation on city buses in Southern cities, beginning with the long and successful boycott led by Rev. Martin Luther King, Jr., against the Montgomery, Alabama, bus system.

During the fifties the movement of population from the cities to the suburbs greatly accelerated. Quiet villages on railroad lines or new superhighways swelled in population and experienced building booms as they became bedroom towns for commuting husbands. The rush to the open spaces opened new business opportunities: the makers and distributors of garden supplies and power lawn mowers flourished; so did producers of patio and barbecue equipment, builders of swimming pools, and other suppliers of goods and services demanded by the new suburbanites. Retailers followed their market out of the city. Just as the supermarket had been a major development of the 1930's, so the shopping center marked the 1950's. The suburban housewife no longer needed to drive into the crowded center of town, but could find space for her station wagon in an ample parking lot and then take her children from grocery supermarket to pharmacy to dress shop to department store with a minimum of time and effort—and then, if she wished, meet a friend for lunch at the Cozy Corner Tea Shop, still in the same shopping center.

The move of people and shops to the suburbs meant, of course, that they were leaving the city, and the effects on downtown areas were increasingly serious. The tax base of large cities shrank; municipal governments became less and less able to provide all needed services; crime and welfare problems increased because those remaining in the cities tended to include a greater proportion of the poor and the uneducated; and there was worried talk of crisis in the cities.

The great interstate highway system was begun in 1956. This program to modernize and expand America's highways called for a road network that would tie together 90 per cent of all cities with more than fifty thousand population as well as thousands of smaller towns, that would make it possible to travel, even across country, without stopping for traffic lights, and that would greatly speed up traffic. Such a program could not fail to have a great impact on America, and its effects went far beyond making driving from one point to another easier and faster. Highways and sprawling interchanges gobbled up vast amounts of land. Initially, many highway planners were given an almost free hand because they represented the magic word "progress," and they often exercised their power with an arrogant disregard for all other values, driving their highways through scenic areas, parks, historic sites, residential areas, and even cemeteries. In time, organized citizen groups, working through public opinion and the courts, were often able to force relocation of highways that threatened to damage neighborhoods or park land. But even where the superhighways were planned with some regard for aesthetics and human values, they permanently changed the face of the land wherever they passed.

During the 1950's another of the diseases that afflict mankind was conquered. Poliomyelitis is a disease that is especially terrifying because it most often attacks children, and it almost always leaves its victims crippled in some way. For some reason polio had become more prevalent during the 1940's, and the rates had remained high—so high that many parents began to dread the coming of summer, the season when the disease struck. In 1954 Dr. Jonas Salk introduced a new polio vaccine in a nationwide test among almost two million schoolchildren; it proved so successful that a campaign was begun to have it given to every child. The polio rate dropped dramatically, from almost twenty-four per one hundred thousand population in 1954 to less than two by 1959—and later much lower.

Another advance in the field of medicine was the first successful kidney transplant in 1954. There was no problem of rejection because the donor was an identical twin, but during the following years hundreds of kidney transplants would be made, and with increasing success, even where the donors were unrelated. Unfortunately, medical science's increasing knowledge of how to deal with the problem of rejection of foreign bodies applied mainly to kidney transplants; the transplanting of other organs was to remain a more difficult problem.

One other health note: in 1954 the American Cancer Society released a report, based on a massive statistical study of smokers and nonsmokers, that indicated that cigarette smokers are many times more likely to be lung cancer victims than are their friends who do not indulge. Cigarette sales fell off somewhat, and many people switched to filter tips, but within a few weeks cigarette sales were just about what they had been before the report was issued.

There was considerable consternation in the United States when the Russians put the first artificial satellite into orbit around the earth in 1959. An American satellite was launched a few months later, but it was much smaller than the Russian sputnik. The situation was not a happy one for Americans who had been sure of their technological superiority, and it took a major national effort to assure that the United States would not continue to play second fiddle in space.

American-Made Drums . . .

24 25 26 **American Dance Band Equipment.** Chrome-plated hardware. Instruction book. Shipped from Buffalo, N.Y. Factory —allow 7 days extra.
State color: White Pearl or Sparkle finish in Blue, Gold, Silver or Black.

F **Souffle-Pouf** . . . feminine drama, romantically yours in delicately patterned Acetate and Nylon lace. Styled for sophisticated glamour with its appealing bateau neck (scooped in back) and long, wrist-length sleeves.

DB2954–Pay $2.00 down or Cash. $19.98

STEVEN DEUTCH

A RESTLESS NATION

Some old patterns of American life had been shaken up during World War II, and the tide of change was running hard during the 1950's. For one thing, the big cities had lost much of their appeal for many people, and the trend was to leave the metropolises and move to the suburbs. Also, the population had become much more mobile, and by the fifties it was a rare person who expected to live in the same house all, or even most, of his life. At left is a Los Angeles neighborhood in 1954 on May 1, a traditional moving day; it appears that almost everyone is going somewhere else. Above is a suburban outdoor art show. Suburban communities, blessed with much resident talent, organized a busy schedule of cultural activities.

Suburban living means that one must commute to the city to work, and some breadwinners wonder at times if the gain is worth the price. The Chicago commuters above travel by train; elsewhere it might be by bus or private automobile. Nor did young wives like the one at the right find that a nice house and a modern kitchen necessarily meant bliss: babies still cried and cakes burned.

THE ORGANIZATION CHILD

By the fifties no community was complete without its full schedule of Little League baseball and Pop Warner football, swimming lessons, tennis tournaments, and other organized activities for youngsters. True, some of these were not new, but "supervised recreation" for kids did not become of major importance to parents till the postwar period. Above, a coach in Ponca City, Oklahoma, gives his young team the word. At right, Boy Scouts march in a Fourth of July parade in York, Pennsylvania.

OVERLEAF: A different and less organized kind of sport in a setting now vanishing: local sages argue weighty matters in a South Carolina general store.

298

YOUTH IN THE FIFTIES

Except for a reluctance to become involved in events, the youth of the 1950's were fairly average young men and women. Their music was rock 'n' roll, especially as performed by Elvis Presley, and like the group above, they liked to gather in basement playrooms to talk, dance, and consume soft drinks (alcohol, not drugs, was the problem of suburbia and the campus). The couple at left illustrate a curious trend among high school pupils of the period—the abandonment of casual dating in favor of "going steady." Some psychologists explained it as a seeking for security. The group at right are at a fraternity party; the crew cut was big among college men during those years.

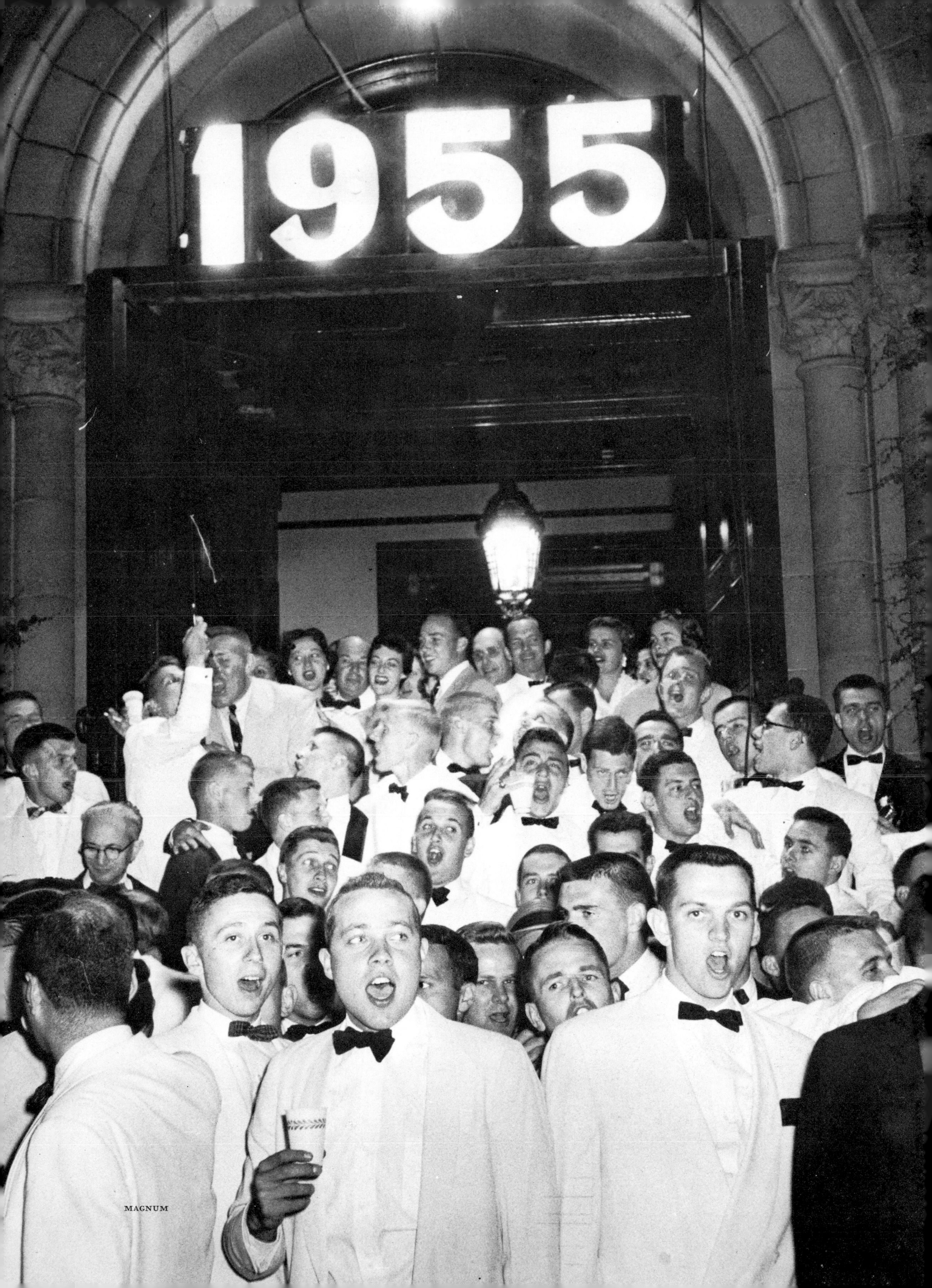

MAGNUM

THE COLLEGE CROWD

The Korean War brought more veterans into colleges under the GI Bill of Rights, but the postwar domination of campuses by veterans was ending. All-female Vassar had few veterans, though there may have been one or two former WAC's or WAVES among the girls above carrying the traditional daisy chain in 1953. The balcony climbers at top right are Tufts College men making a pantie raid on the girls of adjoining Jackson College in Massachusetts in 1952. The girls often cooperated in such madness; this time they doused the raiders with perfumed water. The circular picture at the right shows a brief-lived college lunacy: goldfish-swallowing. At bottom right, in a San Francisco coffee house, are beatniks, members of the beat generation, who rejected contemporary ideas of morality, dress, and behavior.

304

DAVID R. PHILLIPS

Not everyone joined in the population exodus from the inner cities to the suburbs. Most could not afford to move; but a great many remained because the city offered excitement, stimulation, and cultural advantages. At left, boys in a poor section of New York cool off at an open hydrant. Above, a small girl swings against the backdrop of a big-city housing project.

OVERLEAF: *A group enjoys a Greenwich Village café. The suburbs offered few amenities like this, nor did most of them have first-rate ballet, symphonies, art galleries, and museums.*

307

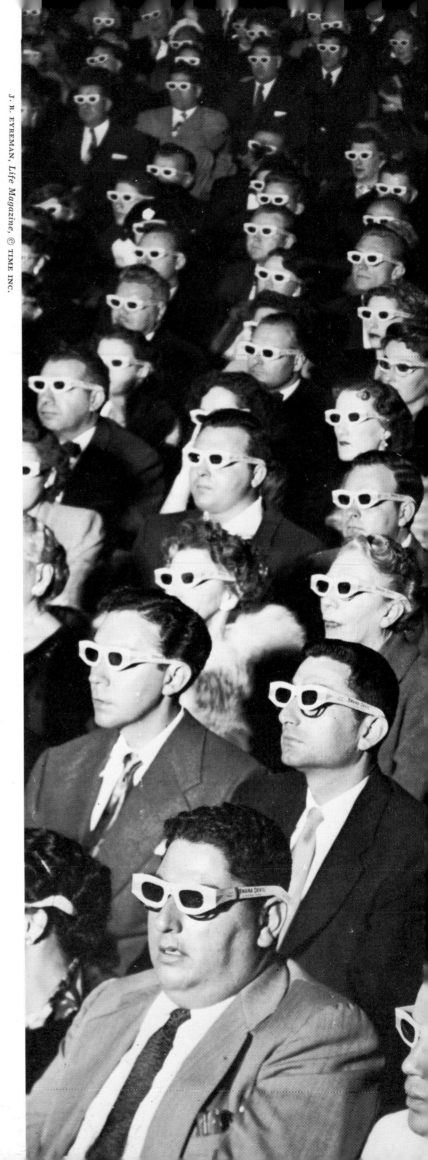

J. R. EYREMAN, *Life Magazine*, © TIME INC.

AT THE MOVIES

Looking like some assembly of weird other-world creatures, these goggled people are watching a three-dimensional movie, an art form that had a brief flowering in the fifties. It did little to revive the film industry, however; in a decade when all other forms of recreation were booming, motion picture attendance continued to sag, from sixty million in 1950 to forty-two million in 1959. Television was keeping people at home.

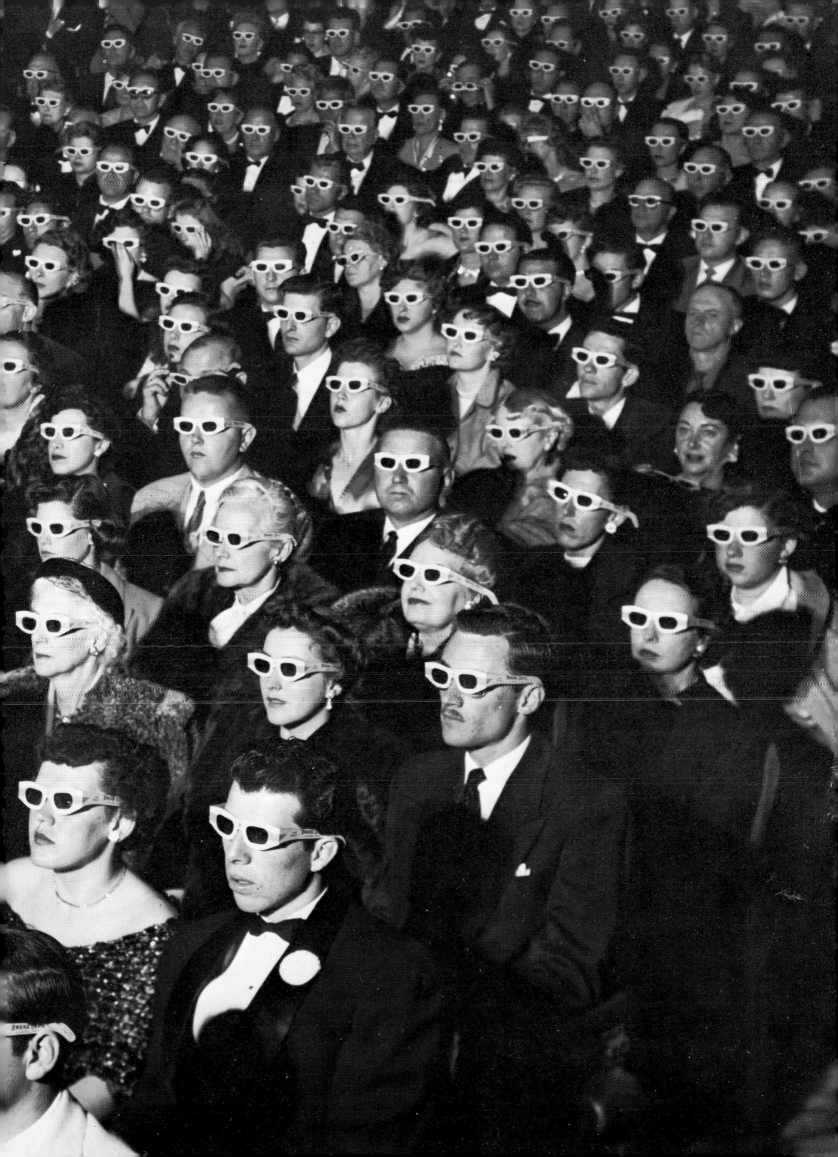

Along with the move to suburbia went a more relaxed and informal style of outdoor living. At top left a mother feeds the neighborhood children with a minimum of fuss on barbecued hamburgers and frankfurters. "Planned obsolescence" became a catchword in the 1950's, and the auto makers promoted it with distinctive annual changes in body styling. At lower left an automobile with fender fins—a styling innovation of the period—is photographed in juxtaposition with a woman in a chemise dress and spike heels—passing women's fashions of the moment. The hula hoop was a tremendously popular fad of the late fifties; the young lady below, at a party in Columbia, South Carolina, in 1958, hulaed so vigorously that she twirled her panties right off.

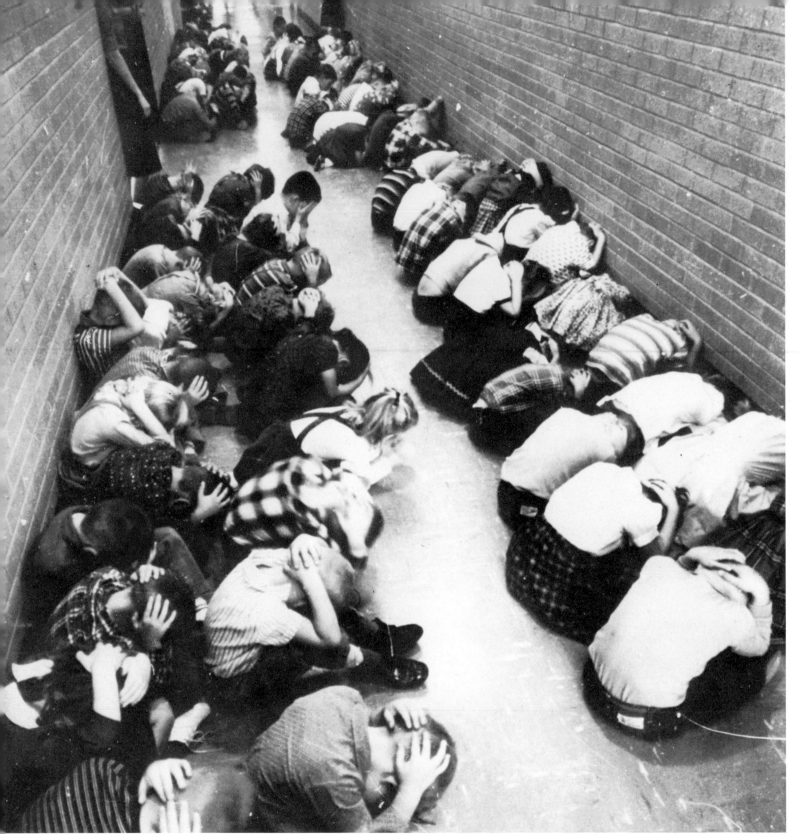

ON GROWING UP

A middle-class child of the 1950's seemed to be growing up in a period when there was every reason to be happy, but childhood then was no easier than in other times. Educators were trying new theories on youngsters, child psychologists had conflicting ideas about the best way to rear them, and no child could remain untouched by the tensions affecting his parents. The schoolchildren above are holding an air raid drill; a Russian attack was still considered possible. Some things, though, remained timeless; the boys at right fishing by a covered bridge in Pennsylvania could have been photographed half a century earlier.

GRANT HEILMAN

STEVEN DEUTCH

The impact of the automobile on American life became greater than ever during the fifties. The interstate highway program, begun in 1956, was soon not only producing strips of limited-access, high-speed, nonstop roadway, but changing countryside and city where it passed. In 1950 Americans drove their cars, trucks, and buses a little more than four hundred fifty million miles; ten years later they rolled up seven hundred million miles. By 1959 there were seventy-one million motor vehicles on the road, and parking was such a serious problem that the multilevel garage had become a common architectural form in many cities. At left such a structure creates a striking geometric design with its tier upon tier of gleaming chrome-fronted automobiles.

Crowds in Grand Central Station watch on television the launch of Gordon Cooper's 1968 earth-orbiting flight. At right, a policeman stands guard at Columbia University during the 1968 campus riots.

318

THE RESTLESS YEARS: 1960-72

Electric Guitars

134^{95}
No Money Down

Strap Incl. with (N)

84^{95}
No Money Down

It is easy enough to chronicle the events since 1960; it is more difficult to get at their meanings. We are still too close to those events to obtain a perspective; moreover, many of the dramas are still being played, and there is no way yet of knowing how or when the last act will end.

As descriptive an appellation as any for the period is "the restless years," for the time seemed to have more than its share of concern, disquiet, and even open violence. People debated and were often bitterly divided over the war in Vietnam, the generation gap, racial integration, marijuana, women's liberation, abortion, and a number of other matters big and small. Some of the controversies were probably magnified out of proportion now and then by the press and television, but there is no doubt that these times tended to be tense and volatile.

The nation continued prosperous, as it had since World War II, with the exception of places such as Appalachia, where poverty had become an unhappy way of life. The sound of the builder's hammer was heard across the land, not only trying to keep ahead of the demand of a growing population for dwellings, but also erecting skyscrapers in every major city. Automobiles, appliances, clothing, recreation equipment— the public was buying freely. But it was not a completely balanced economy, for wages and prices rose with discomforting regularity, caus-ing housewives to wring their hands at check-out counters and to join from time to time in sporadic angry but largely ineffectual buyers' strikes. Then, to compound the problem, a business recession occurred at the end of the sixties, and the nation had the spectacle of simulta-

319

neous unemployment and inflation, a state of affairs that brought limited government controls beginning in late 1971.

The inflation was caused mainly by the war in Vietnam; the United States was producing a huge amount of war goods in addition to full production of civilian goods. But the war in Indochina went deeper than economies: it was affecting the fiber of the nation, and many of America's other ailments were traceable to the conflict half a world away. Americans had been quite generally approving when President Kennedy first sent "advisers" to help the South Vietnamese army. But as years passed the advisers had become divisions of combat troops, the casualty lists had mounted, and victory remained elusive. The first to become widely disillusioned were the young of draft age. There were demonstrations on college campuses and before the gates of military installations; young men burned their draft cards, fled to Canada, went to prison rather than serve in a war they considered immoral. A climax came in 1968 with the destructive and violent riots at Columbia University in New York, which were followed by campus disorders across the country. For a time the protesters were largely college youths, and they were severely criticized for their lack of patriotism, but as the war went interminably on the balance between hawks and doves gradually shifted. Fewer and fewer Americans asked for victory; more and more wished only to end the conflict.

The young generation was a far cry from the sports-jacketed, crew-cut conformists of the 1950's. Young men in college and even in high school grew beards, mustaches, and sideburns, and let their hair go uncut and sometimes unkempt. As for young girls, they too let their hair grow long, but it had to be lank. Both sexes adopted nondescript clothing: old jackets, faded blue jeans, sandals or moccasins. This was not necessarily universal, but it was pretty much the accepted costume of the youth culture. Sociologists interpreted it as a sign of revolt by middle-class youth against the materialism of their parents and of American society. There were many observers who could not resist pointing out that the same young people were perfectly willing to accept motorcycles, automobiles, and other products of the materialistic society they professed to despise.

Among a part of the youth of the time, the revolt against society took the form of the hippie movement, in which the person simply "copped out" or refused to contribute anything to society. True hippies refused to work, slept where they could, begged food. They called themselves flower children and believed that universal love was the solution to all their problems. Though it existed in many parts of the country, their strange subculture had its spiritual center—if such a term as "spiritual" can be used—in the Haight-Ashbury section of San Francisco. Their way of life was not conducive to hygienic living; worse yet, they encouraged the use of drugs: marijuana, the dangerous, psychedelic LSD, and deadly methedrine, or "speed." However, the cult of the hippies faded before the 1960's ended; flower children could not live in a harsh world, and soon the once-teeming streets of Haight-Ashbury had gone back to a seedy, nondescript state.

320

Most middle-class youngsters, of college age and even younger, had had a great deal of freedom to come and go, not only because parental control had been weakened but because parental money was available to them in generous amounts. During the middle sixties the thing to do among college students was to go to Florida beaches, especially Fort Lauderdale, on their spring vacations, and they congregated annually by tens of thousands from all over the nation at a cost that was far from insignificant. Then in 1968 youth's expression of its identity took a new turn with the huge Woodstock Rock Festival in New York State. Rock festivals proliferated, and young people flocked to them like migrating lemmings, proclaiming that rock music was the authentic sound of the liberated young. Some of the festivals were ill-planned, with inadequate arrangements for food, water, and housing. The craze wore itself out; the last gasp came in 1971 near McCrea, Louisiana, where the crowd stood about in the open sun in temperatures that went above 100 degrees. There were no more rock festivals.

Yet it was not all fun and games and irresponsibility for the young. A great many, especially those preparing for professional careers, took their college too seriously to have time for lying around the Fort Lauderdale beach. It was largely the young who did the doorbell ringing and other volunteer work for Senator Eugene McCarthy in the New Hampshire primary in 1968, a crucial contest whose result convinced President Johnson that he should not seek re-election. The young were activists in environmental and antipollution work and in other social causes. In recognition of their early maturity and responsibility, the voting age was lowered to eighteen years in 1971.

Space exploration was one of the exciting continuing stories of the era. The Soviet Union put the first man into space, made the longest flights, was the first with a two-man flight—in fact, led in virtually every statistic and category. But by 1965 the balance began to tip the other way, and American supremacy was established beyond all doubt when American astronauts stepped out on the surface of the moon on July 20, 1969.

There was some grumbling about the space program—notably the complaint that so much effort and such huge sums of money could better be spent to alleviate social ills—but those voices were a small minority, and most Americans were proud and well content with the moon landings. Nevertheless, there were problems crying for solution. For one, there was the matter of drugs; one of the saddest developments of the period was the growth of drug addiction. It was not so much the relatively mild marijuana, which the young appeared to be using much as their parents used alcohol, but rather the addictive drugs, especially heroin. Cases of addiction even among junior high school students had become not uncommon. Drugs were also responsible in part for a rising urban crime rate; a drug habit is very expensive to support, and the addict often resorts to burglary, armed robbery, mugging, or prostitution to obtain money.

Race relations, too, remained a pressing matter and became an area of active confrontation during the sixties. In 1960 young blacks began

B **Automatic Frypan—Now Stainless Steel Inside** for easiest washing. Bonded to aluminum pan for fast, even heat conduction. 2-position lid— use LOW to prevent spatter; HIGH to stir, serve. Turn lid upside down with one hand by Tip n' See handle. Braising leg for fat-free frying.

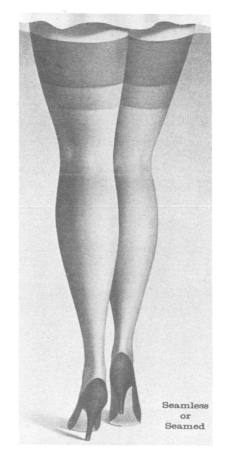

Seamless **$149** PR. LOTS OF 6

Daytime Sheers. Extra roominess with these 30 Denier Nylons. A sure way to fashionable no-seam leg glamour, comfort.

sit-ins at lunch counters in the South in peaceful demands for the right to be served. In other actions Negroes pressed for the right to vote. They were often answered with shootings from ambush, bombings of their churches, and other outrages. For some young blacks non-violence was too slow, and the Black Power movement came into being, demanding action at once. The most militant acts, however, occurred in the North, where on several occasions frustrated blacks, angered by poverty, unemployment, and confinement to the ghetto, engaged in violent rioting, first in the Watts district of Los Angeles in 1965, and followed over the next three years or so by outbreaks in Cleveland, Detroit, Newark, Harlem, and Washington, D.C. On the other hand, blacks began to make use of their political muscle and elected mayors of three large Northern cities (Cleveland, Newark, Gary) and a number of local officials as well as a state legislator in the Deep South.

For the first time the general public became acutely aware of pollution and the environment. Farseeing men have long recognized that the resources of this land are not unlimited—it was just a century ago, in 1872, that Congress created our first national park, Yellowstone, to preserve its marvels for posterity—yet the idea that even the vastness of the sky and the oceans could be corrupted seemed preposterous. But with a rapidly growing population and proliferating industry, many lakes and rivers became hazards to health, and the air over some cities at times was turned into an eye-smarting smog. Today we recognize that a problem exists, but we have not yet reached the stage of concerted action. There has been some progress. Many communities now ban all outdoor burning of trash; even the nostalgic odor of leaves burning in the autumn is becoming a thing of the past. Stricter emissions standards have been set for automobiles. Manufacturers are now subject to heavy fines for pollution instead of being slapped on the wrist. There is a long way to go before waters as heavily polluted as those of Lake Erie are sparkling blue and clean again, but a small start has been made.

The opposite side of the coin of pollution is awareness of the total environment, and this period saw a tremendous increase in the number of people enjoying the open spaces. Some did it the easy way: the highways in any vacation region in summer were one long parade of campers and motor homes of all sizes and degrees of elaborateness. These people, however, were scorned by the rugged backpackers who fanned out into the forests and mountains on foot trails. The backpackers are a numerous fraternity today; a dozen years ago they were still only a small band. So great was the number of people trying to see outdoor America that some of the national parks were strained almost beyond capacity, and future policy will discourage the use of private automobiles in some parks.

The term "population explosion" came into popular use during this period. Though the problem is much more acute in some other parts of the world, even in the United States the average American realized, as the traffic jams grew ever bigger and the housing developments spread over the meadows where he had played as a boy, that an ever-increasing number of human beings was somehow diluting the quality of American life. Planned parenthood organizations and zero population growth advocates argued for a limitation on births. There were those on the other side who claimed that the nation could support much more than its present population and that continued growth meant economic health. Regardless of the arguments pro and con, it appeared that the problem might be on the way to settling itself. Though the population of the United States had increased from about 180 million in 1960 to 203 million in 1970, the increase was less than had been predicted. The rate of growth was slowing down, much below what demographers had projected. If it continued its decline, it might well soon reach a point of zero population growth.

The census of 1970 revealed other things besides the number of people in the country. It showed, for one thing, that the move from farm to urban areas was continuing. Less than one person in twenty was still on the farm; at the first census in 1790 the proportions had been just about reversed. But the cities had not necessarily been gaining population, for the middle class—almost entirely white—had been moving to the suburbs. As a result, the proportion of minority groups in the inner cities rose; in some Northern cities—Washington, Newark —they came to outnumber whites. There was also a broad movement toward the West and the South; the sunshine states of Florida, California, and Arizona had large gains in population; in states such as the Dakotas, where agriculture was the main industry and where modern methods made fewer people necessary to cultivate the soil, population increase was very small.

In the field of science and technology, the computer was king during much of the period. The public marveled at the ability of an electronics system to guide a vehicle down to a landing on the moon and then cursed computers when they tried to get a billing error corrected. In the field of medicine, discoveries included the Sabin oral vaccine against polio, more effective even than the Salk vaccine. The first heart transplant was done in South Africa in 1967 and was followed by scores of similar operations in the United States. Though the techniques were beyond reproach, the body in almost every instance eventually rejected the transplanted heart. Surgeons attempted lung, liver, and pancreas transplants; failure was total. One development of the time with deep social implications was the contraceptive pill, released in 1960 after five years of testing. Though condemned by the Roman Catholic Church, it offered the first almost foolproof method of family planning. There were some who suggested that it might also give further permissiveness to the already liberal moral standards of youth.

The Selma march was a dramatic episode in the civil rights struggles of the sixties. Protected by a court order that forbade interference by state officials or others, participants walked from Selma to

324

Montgomery, Alabama, a five-day trip, to demonstrate for voting and other rights. Led by Martin Luther King, Jr., the blacks were joined by many whites, including clergymen and nuns.

EXPERIENCES OF YOUTH

The youth of the period were moved by varied philosophies. The hippie above at a New York Central Park "Be-In" was one of the flower children who believed love would change the world; most learned that it was not so simple. The confrontation at the left is between a policeman and a Madison, Wisconsin, antiwar protester.

OVERLEAF: The generation gap is apparent as young people at the 1970 Goose Lake, Michigan, Rock Festival get a critical and thorough inspection from elders.

THE THINKING MACHINES

Automation and computerization expanded their scope and capabilities tremendously during the sixties. Many factories became almost entirely automated, and computers were programmed to perform such varied tasks as guiding spacecraft, setting type for books, controlling city traffic, and aiding in the medical diagnosis of disease. A relatively simple application of automation is pictured above: a machine performs a series of operations on an airplane part. The operator does little more than keep an eye on things. At right, pupils in a Brooklyn school are receiving individualized instruction from a computer located in Manhattan. When the picture was made in 1968, the same computer gave reading and spelling lessons to six thousand pupils, was used after hours for adult education classes, and processed administrative data for the New York City Board of Education.

330

UNITED PRESS INTERNATIONAL

A PEOPLE'S MARKET

The open shopping center, usually built around two or three sides of a large parking lot, had been the ultimate in convenience for a motorized public, but in the sixties newer and better ways to attract and serve shoppers were being tried. This is a view of the inside of a multilevel enclosed shopping center at Mount Prospect, Illinois. Opened in 1962 by three large department stores, it also has seventy-five smaller shops as well as professional offices.

THE AFFLUENT SOCIETY

Despite an inflated economy, more Americans had more money and leisure during the sixties and early seventies than ever before. The five-day week was universal, and some firms were introducing a four-day work week; the month-long vacation was common. And wages were high enough to allow blue-collar workers to enjoy their vacations as easily—and often at the same places—as executives. At the right, lying in rows to bake in the Florida sun, are 1967 winter vacationers at a Miami Beach hotel. The man above, casting for fish in a Colorado lake, is one of a great company of owners of motor homes or campers. Few recreational items have gained so in popularity in recent years despite a rather high price tag.

OVERLEAF: The young also shared the general affluence (always excepting the unfortunate). Where kids once danced to record players, they now had combos at parties, and in some quarters a sports car was a common high school graduation gift.

334

WIDE WORLD

GENE DANIELS, BLACK STAR

At the left, downtown Los Angeles lies shrouded in smog. Such pollution—of earth and water as well as air—aroused increasing concern during the sixties and increased popular interest in protection of the environment. The women above are picketing in 1964 against a proposed incinerator at Oyster Bay on Long Island, on the grounds that its smoke and fumes would pollute the air.

Fashions during the period tended to show less fabric and more woman. The miniskirts at the right are 1960 versions, when the style was new on the scene; they soon stopped looking like hoopskirts for midgets. The young lady walking in the rain above wears hot pants, the latest brevity in 1971. At the other extreme during the era were the popular pants suits, which covered everything from neck to shin.

MONKMEYER PRESS PHOTOS

THE CONFUSED COLLEGIAN

It is impossible to generalize about the college youth of this period. Depending on the particular student and the year, they were lackadaisical or studious, conservative or radical, noninvolved or activist. They made their greatest impact on the awareness of the nation during the late 1960's with an outbreak of demonstrations, some violent, against the war in Vietnam, but this was only one episode in a college generation as restless as that of the previous decade had been even-tempered. At the left is one of their less edifying activities, a student gathering at Fort Lauderdale, Florida, in 1964. During most of the sixties it was a strange annual rite for students from universities across the country to assemble on the beaches at Fort Lauderdale and nearby towns for their spring vacation. Above is a more serious side of college life: a married student studies at home late at night.

343

DON RUTLEDGE, BLACK STAR

TO FIND ONE'S SELF

Tensions mount and mental problems increase as our society grows ever more complex, and Americans, in their search for self-identity and relief from neuroses, turned in some strange directions during the 1960's, to everything from encounter groups to self-styled gurus imparting Oriental wisdom. The young people at left are members of the Jesus movement being baptized in the ocean at Long Beach, California. Youth, so often confused and purposeless, rediscovered religion about 1970, and large numbers embraced it with fervor. At the Esalen Institute in California devotees experimented with encounter groups, massage, and meditation in a search for new levels of awareness. The participants above are practicing yoga on a cliff overlooking the Pacific at sunset.

OVERLEAF: Another time-tested therapy for relieving anxieties is to get near nature. This family is in Cathedral Pines Park in northwestern Connecticut.

A workman, above, clambers over one of R. Buckminster Fuller's geodesic domes. At right is an artist's rendering of a manned, earth-orbiting space station, one of several types proposed by NASA.

Epilogue

NASA

Much has happened in these United States during this past American century. The winds of change have blown hard; the barest catalogue of the differences between now and a hundred years ago could fill volumes.

Much of our land was empty a hundred years ago; there were only thirty-seven states at the beginning of the 1870's. Our population has increased many-fold; there were not quite 39 million of us at the 1870 census; there were 203 million in 1970.

We were pretty much a farm and village nation a hundred years back. In 1870 the census bureau recorded three out of four Americans as rural people, a category that included not only farmers but also those who lived in hamlets or villages of 2,500 people or less. Today only one out of five of us lives in such quiet spots, and fewer than one in twenty lives on a farm. Not that there is less farmland: fewer people are farming more land.

The changes in living style over the same century have been almost too great to comprehend. The household of a hundred years ago had no such electrically powered servants as toasters, mixers, washing machines, vacuum cleaners. It was the strong arms of the mistress of the house and her daughters that kneaded the bread dough, wrung out the wash, beat the carpets, and did innumerable other chores that are today done by machines.

Central heating, that pervasive warmth that we take so for granted today, was almost unknown a century (and much less) ago. In city or on farm, the kitchen range and a heating stove or two kept the cold at bay, and it was a major job to keep them stoked, especially in the depths of a northern winter. Every home had its woodshed or coal bin; an onerous chore of boyhood was keeping the wood box or coal scuttle filled and the ashes emptied.

The differences between city and rural life a hundred years back were less marked than they are now, for cities then were, basically, overgrown small towns. Buildings seldom rose more than half a dozen stories (we lacked the architectural know-how, the materials, and the adequate passenger elevators required for skyscrapers), there were no apartment houses, and the single-family dwelling was the rule in the city as in the country. Soon the city man might be living slightly more cramped in two- or three-family dwellings, but he could usually boast of gas lights in his home, whereas rural homes were lighted only by the yellow gleam of kerosene lamps. The great majority of city people, like their rural cousins, took their Saturday night baths in a laundry tub in the kitchen and had a privy in the back yard. The horse was virtually the only means of private travel, and in cities it was the prime mover for public transport—horsecars, buses, hansom cabs.

It was not long before the processes of urbanization began to put a much wider gap between the city man and the villager and farmer. Advancing technology soon made indoor plumbing the rule rather than the exception in cities. Architects learned how to erect skyscrapers and how to design apartment houses. Electricity introduced labor-saving devices into the home and powered the trolley, which not only made it easier to get around the city but also gave rise to the suburbs and to the commuter.

Most of these changes passed the rural areas by. The back country still lived in an isolation that became total when bad weather closed the poor roads. A farmer had to come to town for his mail or do without until 1896, when the post office began its first rural free delivery routes; even then the farmer could not get a package delivered to his mailbox until parcel post service came into being in 1913. Not until the arrival of the flivver before the First World War did the farmer's world begin to change; then he and his family could get away from the farm more often and could go farther more quickly. But evening chores called them back at the end of the day, and things at home were pretty much the same; the farmer's wife still carried water from the pump in a bucket and heated it on the kitchen range for the family washing. Only within the last two or three decades, with widespread rural electrification, have the majority of farms acquired gas or oil heat, running water, a flush toilet, and an electric refrigerator. The irony is that although life down on the farm has become more comfortable, there are fewer farm families to enjoy it.

Other changes and developments are beyond counting. A third of a century ago railroad passenger travel was still in its great days; since then it has become a pale ghost, done in by the automobile and the airplane, and it is still too early to know whether present efforts to revive passenger service will succeed. The trolley was another victim of the automobile. Although some streetcars still operate in a few cities, their service is a far cry from the 1920's, when more than thirteen billion passengers in America rode the streetcars in a peak year, and it was even possible to charter an open-air car for a summer trolley party.

We have changed in philosophies as well as in tangibles. Formerly a citizen had no economic security in time of trouble; today we have come to believe that society has certain responsibilities to its members. The discharged worker has unemployment insurance to tide him over, the old have social security, and the impoverished can turn to welfare for help. The system is not perfect; it may have shortcomings and there are abuses, but there have been advances over the bleak and grudging asylum of the old-time county poor farm. In line with this philosophy of taking care of our fellow citizens, we also enforce child labor laws, legislation to outlaw sweatshops, laws to insure safe working conditions. Yet there was a day when the Supreme Court consistently ruled that such measures were unconstitutional.

We have also witnessed a far-reaching change in the condition of the black man in America, most of it since World War II. There is room for a great deal more improvement, especially in the attitudes and subtle discrimination that legislation cannot reach, but the days when Negroes stepped off the sidewalk in the South to make way for a white man are well behind us. Opportunities are far from equal yet, but the gap is slowly closing.

Another quite spectacular change has been in the status of women. Through the Victorian era, and even after, man was the lord and master, woman the subservient creature who existed to wait on him and to bear his children. Early suffragettes and advocates of women's rights were objects of masculine ridicule as well as scorn by many of their own sex. Nevertheless, their truth went marching on: not only did women get the vote (which did not purify the nation's politics the way they had predicted it would), but they also came into possession of a number of other privileges that had been exclusively male.

As new life styles evolve around new social conditions and scientific discoveries, new attitudes develop to defend or deplore these changes. Thus new individual behavioral codes have become the subjects of legislative debate and public controversy. In time, of course, and in the American tradition of frantic experimentation with alternate amounts of too much pepper and too much salt, new values will emerge from our cultural caldron. Perhaps the "nostalgic" appeal of this book is a sign that despite the present cultural ferment, what was good about the "good old days" has been preserved in the American consciousness. And while over a century we have lost some of the things that were good, we also do well to count up our gains, for they are many.

On the Sound Magazine, CURTIS KAUFMAN

In launching the era of the American Bicentennial in 1970, the President proclaimed that the goal for our nation in the 1970's is "to forge a new national commitment, a new spirit of '76, a spirit which vitalizes the ideals for which the Revolution was fought, a spirit which will unite the nation in purpose and dedication to the advancement of human welfare as it moves into its third century."

Improvement of the quality of life—that is the challenge of our next American century.